Revival Sermons

— *of* —

JONATHAN EDWARDS

Revival Sermons

of

JONATHAN EDWARDS

Revival Sermons of Jonathan Edwards

© 2017 Hendrickson Publishers Marketing, LLC
P. O. Box 3473
Peabody, Massachusetts 01961-3473
www.hendrickson.com

ISBN 978-1-61970-909-6

Originally published by Hendrickson Publishers in *Sermons of Jonathan Edwards*.

Printed in the United States of America

First Printing — March 2017

Cover image: This work is in the public domain.

Contents

Preface

Jonathan Edwards (1703–1758)

The kind of religion that God requires, and will accept, does not consist in weak, dull, and lifeless "wouldings"—those weak inclinations that lack convictions—that raise us but a little above indifference. God, in his word, greatly insists that we be in good earnest, fervent in spirit, and that our hearts be engaged vigorously in our religion: "Be fervent in spirit, serving the Lord" (Romans 12:11).

—Jonathan Edwards, *A Treatise Concerning Religious Affections* (1746)

For most twenty-first century Americans, Jonathan Edwards is a murky figure from the distant past. Most will recognize that he was a preacher, a few might remember his connections with colonial New England. And some might even associate him with the Great Awakening, the first spiritual revival in North America.

In fact, Jonathan Edwards is considered one of this country's greatest theologians, a thinker and philosopher who had a prophetic grasp of the impact that Enlightenment thinking and scientific endeavor would have on Christian thought and experience.

His Times

Edwards was born just eight-three years after the Mayflower found safe haven in Plymouth Harbor on the western side of Cape Cod Bay in Massachusetts. Fewer than half of the 102 passengers on that famous voyage were English Separatists—those who sought to purify the established Church of England, and for their efforts were persecuted and forced out of England. Known as Puritans, it was their faith and values that were codified in the Mayflower Compact, and ultimately became the foundation of New England civil code and the very fabric of society and life in New England.

For a moment, imagine the times. When Jonathan Edwards lived, the colonies in America were not united. In fact, they were separated by religion and politics and countries of origin. Each colony had its own distinct values and laws, its own immigrant populations, its own industry and commerce. New England was just that: New *England*. They were English people intent on creating a godly commonwealth in a new land—the sort of government and society unavailable to them in England.

When Edwards lived, the colonies were tethered to Europe, England mostly, and those ties were tested repeatedly. Sometimes those ties were tightly reined in by English troops and governors intent on maintaining control of the colonies and garnering as much revenue for the Crown as possible. In other periods, the colonies seemed to be left to their own devices, to set up their own government and make their own decisions.

In 1700, the European population in all the American colonies was two hundred and fifty thousand; ninety-one thousand of whom lived in New England. By 1775, the population of the colonies had increased to two and a half million. During Edwards' lifetime, the colonies experienced considerable growth with all its attendant pressures and difficulties, particularly in New England, where everything—its values, its laws, its very society—was defined and designed in the light of Puritan Christianity.

There it is again—that word *Puritan*. It is a distorted word today, having come to refer largely to sexual mores that should more honestly be credited to Victorians. Puritan values were about strong families, ethical and moral behavior, and a strong work ethic—and their laws codified the behaviors that were expected of a godly people. While the law can, at least for a time, influence behavior, it cannot guarantee that the hearts of the citizens are righteous. It was no different in New England.

The Massachusetts colony assumed that all settlers were or should be Christian. In fact, it insisted, prohibiting immigrants who were Roman

Catholic or otherwise outside the fold. At the beginning in particular, a good portion of the early settlers came to escape religious persecution. Their faith was vital and personal. After all, nominal faith is unimaginable in a persecuted church. But within the first one hundred years of the colony—by the time Edwards was ready to begin his ministry—the Puritans were no longer the persecuted church; instead they had become the established church, with all its attendant benefits, including power and the tax revenues collected to support the church. And in an established church, nominal faith becomes the norm.

Edwards faced a generation plump and happy with their flourishing businesses and relatively peaceful lives. It was a generation filled with spiritual apathy, materialism, and worldliness, whose spiritual life was far from the vibrant faith of the settlers who had sailed from England just two generations before. Confronting this spiritual apathy would become Edwards' life work.

His Early Life

Jonathan Edwards was born in East Windsor, Connecticut, the fifth of eleven children and the only son—the son and grandson of Congregational pastors. He was a great student, fluent in Hebrew, Greek and Latin by the age of thirteen. He was also gifted in natural science and scientific methodology, and in philosophy. He entered the Collegiate School of Connecticut (later Yale) in 1716 to continue his formal education, and graduated at the head of his class in 1720, then immediately began his divinity studies. He served for a short time as pastor of a Presbyterian church in New York City, then returned to Yale in 1724 to become a senior tutor.

In 1726, Edwards accepted a call from the Congregational church in Northampton, Massachusetts, to serve as assistant pastor to his grandfather, Solomon Stoddard. Stoddard was a highly regarded cleric, a man beloved by his congregants and respected by the Native Americans. Edwards would serve in this church for twenty-three years, long after the death of his grandfather in 1729.

His Family Life

In 1727, Jonathan Edwards married Sarah Pierrepont, a young woman he had met while he was a divinity student at Yale. Their marriage was remarkable by the standards of any age. Jonathan adored his wife Sarah, whom he called "my dear companion." Together, they created a loving home and thriving family, a safe haven where Edwards was able to study and work. Sarah complemented Jonathan; she was practical and socially adept, while he was distracted and intellectual. Theirs was a marriage filled with companionship, lively conversation, and joy. Edwards and Sarah were attentive and available to one another; they nourished one another, enjoyed one another, and valued one another.

Like everything he did, Edwards was intentional about his family life. Jonathan and Sarah had eleven children, who all lived to adulthood. Edwards made his family a priority, routinely spending the hour before dinner each night with the children. When he traveled out of town, Edwards would take one child with him. Often in the afternoon, Edwards and Sarah would set out on horseback where chores and responsibilities would not interrupt their conversation. They each recognized that their family and their relationship were worthy of the same attention given to study or work.

His Ministry

Jonathan Edwards is inseparably linked with the spiritual revival called Great Awakening, for it was under his preaching in Northampton, Massachusetts, that the Awakening came in 1734. Edwards had followed his grandfather Solomon Stoddard as pastor of the Congregational church in Northampton. Stoddard himself was a great revivalist, preaching five successive revivals, but by the time Jonathan took the pulpit in 1729, he discovered the people "very insensible of the things of religion"—their faith was dry and stale and impotent.

There is an irony of sorts in this story. One of the reasons for Stoddard's great popularity is he relaxed church membership requirements: rather than proof of conversion, he opened the sacraments to everyone except those living openly scandalous lives. This "open admission" effectively removed the necessity for an individual personal spiritual experience with Jesus Christ. This policy, although it could be argued as necessary for a society that defined itself only in Christian terms, ultimately served to lead people away from faith, not towards it.

Edwards, on the other hand, had an intimate understanding, both from personal experience and from his studies, that God was knowable, and that it was only in a personal relationship that true "religion" would be found. He began preaching, and while it took several years, by 1733 he began to see change. In 1734, he preached a series on justification by faith, and by the end of that year, the spark had been lit in Northampton.

Revival had been occurring already in New Jersey, through the work of Theodore Frelinghuysen and Gilbert Tennent, encouraging people out of their spiritual lethargy. The message of revival was this: "Outward morality is not enough for salvation. An inward change is necessary." This message is very familiar to the American Protestant ear today, but it was a fresh word to people who had depended on their morality, their outwards actions, their conformation to "Christian" behavior, to secure their place in God's Kingdom.

Revival grew in Northampton, rippling throughout the area and even into neighboring Connecticut. Edwards continued his preaching and God continued blessing. In 1740, the Awakening exploded through the work of Anglican George Whitefield, who arrived in Boston for his second visit to the colonies, this time a six-week evangelistic tour of New England. Edwards was at the center still, but Whitefield became the instrument of expansion, bringing about the most widespread revival that the colonies had ever experienced.

By 1750, the Awakening had receded from public prominence, but it was in this year that Edwards' position with the Northampton church was severed after twenty-three years. The reason? He wanted to change the policy of "open admission" to the sacraments, begun by his grandfather. Edwards' insistence that "only persons who had made a profession of faith could be admitted to the Lord's Supper" enraged his parishioners, and he was asked to leave.

After a few lean months of unemployment, Edwards found a remarkable new work, that of pastor to settlers and missionary to Indians in Stockbridge, a work begun by David Brainerd in the western frontier of Massachusetts. In 1757, he was chosen president of the College of New Jersey (Princeton), and subsequently relocated in order to begin his work, leaving Sarah behind to finish the packing in Stockbridge. A few months after arriving in his new post, a smallpox epidemic broke out, and Edwards chose to receive the new (and risky) inoculation against the disease. Shortly after, he died from complications from that vaccination, on March 22, 1758. His final words in a message to his beloved Sarah were:

Give my kindest love to my dear wife, and tell her that the uncommon union which has so long subsisted between us has been of such a nature as I trust is spiritual and therefore will continue forever.

His Legacy

Though largely associated with the Great Awakening, Edwards leaves a legacy far outside the reach of this remarkable work of God's grace in America. It was Jonathan Edwards who wrestled with the new issues of scientific discovery, the Enlightenment, and the Age of Reason in light of Christian teaching and experience. It was Edwards who faced the emerging climate of humanistic rationalism over the teaching of a personal and loving God. It was Edwards who developed the uniquely American themes of a redeemer nation and a covenant people, a theme that echoes still today in the American mind. It was Edwards who tackled the problem of spiritual deadness by recognizing of the necessity of a personal religious experience and by embracing the supernatural work of the Holy Spirit to awaken and illuminate the heart.

Edwards left a remarkable body of work. He recorded his observations of the Great Awakening in several works, including *A Faithful Narrative of the Surprising Work of God* (1736), in *Distinguishing Marks of a Work of the Spirit of God* (1741) and in *Some Thoughts Concerning the Present Revival of Religion in New England* (1742).

In 1746, he wrote his most famous book, *A Treatise Concerning Religious Affections*. In it he examines the importance of religious "affections" or those "passions that move the will to act," arguing persuasively that true religion resides in the heart, the home of affections, emotions, and inclinations. While in Stockbridge, Edwards completed *Freedom of the Will, and Nature of True Virtue*, and began his massive *History of the Work of Redemption*, which he never completed.

And, of course, Edwards left his sermons. "Sinners in the Hands of an Angry God" (included in this collection) is very likely his best remembered sermon, often used as an example of the Puritan obsession with eternal damnation and a wrathful God. True, it is a call to repentance, one made to a audience who harbored none of this century's distaste and doubts concerning the reality of God's final judgment. However, in fact, this sermon is atypical of Edwards preaching. He spoke more often of God's love and the joys of the Christian life than of the fires of Hell.

Edwards' preaching reflected two of his core beliefs: first, God is the central focus of all religious experience—not humankind or reason or morality. As one writer observes, "Edwards' universe, like his theology, is relentlessly God-centered." And second: knowing God is not merely a rational knowledge—mental assent to particular beliefs—but also a sensible knowledge—experienced, sensed. As the taste of sweetness is distinct from the understanding of sweetness, so a Christian not only believes God is glorious, a Christian also senses the glory of God in his heart.

This collection is a fine sampling of Edwards' sermons during his time in Northampton and Stockbridge. Some are revival sermons, calling for repentance and amendment of life; some are pastoral, some instructional, and others written for specific occasions. But each one is a brilliant and personal invitation to know God both through our intellect and through our affections. These are sermons that challenge our minds, but also, and perhaps more importantly, compel us to open our hearts to the sweet love and joy available to us in our life in Christ.

I am bold in saying this, but I believe that no one is ever changed, either by doctrine, by hearing the Word, or by the preaching or teaching of another, unless the affections are moved by these things. No one ever seeks salvation, no one ever cries for wisdom, no one ever wrestles with God, no one ever kneels in prayer or flees from sin, with a heart that remains unaffected. In a word, there is never any great achievement by the things of religion without a heart deeply affected by those things.

—Jonathan Edwards, *A Treatise Concerning Religious Affections* (1746)

Pardon for the Greatest Sinners

Originally preached between 1734–1739. Also published as "Great Guilt No Obstacle to the Pardon of the Returning Sinner."

"For thy name's sake, O Lord, pardon my iniquity; for it is great."—*Psalm 25:11*

It is evident by some passages in this psalm, that when it was penned, it was a time of affliction and danger with David. This appears particularly by the 15th and following verses: "Mine eyes are ever towards the Lord; for he shall pluck my feet out of the net," etc. His distress makes him think of his sins, and leads him to confess them, and to cry to God for pardon, as is suitable in a time of affliction. See ver. 7. "Remember not the sins of my youth, nor my transgressions;" and verse 18. "Look upon mine affliction, and my pain, and forgive all my sins."

It is observable in the text, what arguments the psalmist makes use of in pleading for pardon.

- *He pleads for pardon for God's name's sake.* He has no expectation of pardon for the sake of any righteousness or worthiness of his for any good deeds he had done, or any compensation he had made for his sins; though if man's righteousness could be a just plea, David would have had as much to plead as most. But he begs that God would do it for his own name's sake, for his own glory, for the glory of his own free grace, and for the honor of his own covenant-faithfulness.

- *The psalmist pleads the greatness of his sins as an argument for mercy.* He not only doth not plead his own righteousness, or the smallness of his sins; he not only doth not say, "Pardon mine iniquity, for I have done much good to counterbalance it"; or,

> Pardon mine iniquity, for it is small, and thou hast no great reason to be angry with me; mine iniquity is not so great, that thou hast any just cause to remember it against me; mine offence is not such but that thou mayest well enough overlook it:

but on the contrary he says, "Pardon mine iniquity, for it is great"; he pleads the greatness of his sin, and not the smallness of it; he enforces his prayer with this consideration, that his sins are very heinous.

> But how could he make this a plea for pardon? I answer, "Because the greater his iniquity was, the more need he had of pardon." It is as much as if he had said,

> Pardon mine iniquity, for it is so great that I cannot bear the punishment; my sin is so great that I am in necessity of pardon; my case will be exceedingly miserable, unless thou be pleased to pardon me.

> He makes use of the greatness of his sin, to enforce his plea for pardon, as a man would make use of the greatness of calamity in begging for relief. When a beggar begs for bread, he will plead the greatness of his poverty and necessity. When a man in distress cries for pity, what more suitable plea can be urged than the extremity of his case? And God allows such a plea as this: for he is moved to mercy towards us by nothing in us but the miserableness of our case. He doth not pity sinners because they are worthy, but because they need his pity.

Doctrine

If we truly come to God for mercy, the greatness of our sin will be no impediment to pardon. If it were an impediment, David would never have used it as a plea for pardon, as we find he does in the text. The following things are needful in order that we truly come to God for mercy.

I. That we should see our misery, and be sensible of our need of mercy.

They who are not sensible of their misery cannot truly look to God for mercy; for it is the very notion [definition] of divine mercy, that it is the goodness and grace of God to the miserable. Without misery in the object, there can be no exercise of mercy. To suppose mercy without supposing misery, or pity without calamity, is a contradiction: therefore men cannot look upon themselves as proper objects of mercy, unless they first know themselves to be miserable; and so, unless this be the case, it is impossible that they should come to God for mercy. They must be sensible that they are the children of wrath; that the law is against them, and that they are exposed to the curse of it: that the wrath of God abideth on them; and that he is angry' with them every day while they are under the guilt of sin. They must be sensible that it is a very dreadful thing to be the object of the wrath of God; that it is a very awful thing to have him for their enemy; and that they cannot bear his wrath. They must be sensible that the guilt of sin makes them miserable creatures, whatever temporal enjoyments they have; that they can be no other than miserable, undone creatures, so long as God is angry with them; that they are without strength, and must perish, and that eternally, unless God help them. They must see that their case is utterly desperate, for anything that anyone else can do for them; that they hang over the pit of eternal misery; and that they must necessarily drop into it, if God have not mercy on them.

II. They must be sensible that they are not worthy, that God should have mercy on them.

They who truly come to God for mercy, come as beggars, and not as creditors: they come for mere mercy, for sovereign grace, and not for anything that is due. Therefore, they must see that the misery under which they lie is justly brought upon them, and that the wrath to which they are exposed is justly threatened against them; and that they have deserved that God should be their enemy, and should continue to be their enemy. They must be sensible that it would be just with God to do as he hath threatened in his holy law, viz. make them the objects of his wrath and curse in Hell to all eternity. They who come to God for mercy in a right manner are not disposed to find fault with his severity; but they come in a sense of their own utter unworthiness, as with ropes about their necks, and lying in the dust at the foot of mercy.

III. They must come to God for mercy in and through Jesus Christ alone.

All their hope of mercy must be from the consideration of what he is, what he hath done, and what he hath suffered; and that there is no other name given under Heaven, among men, whereby we can be saved, but that of Christ; that he is the Son of God, and the Savior of the world; that his blood cleanses from all sin, and that he is so worthy, that all sinners who are in him may well be pardoned and accepted. It is impossible that any should come to God for mercy, and at the same time have no hope of mercy. Their coming to God for it, implies that they have some hope of obtaining it, otherwise they would not think it worth the while to come. But they that come in a right manner have all their hope through Christ, or from the consideration of his redemption, and the sufficiency of it. If persons thus come to God for mercy, the greatness of their sins will be no impediment to pardon. Let their sins be ever so many, and great, and aggravated, it will not make God in the least degree more backward to pardon them. This may be made evident by the following considerations:

1. *The mercy of God is as sufficient for the pardon of the greatest sins, as for the least; and that because his mercy is infinite.* That which is infinite, is as much above what is great, as it is above what is small. Thus God being infinitely great, he is as much above kings as he is above beggars; he is as much above the highest angel, as he is above the meanest worm. One finite measure doth not come any nearer to the extent of what is infinite than another. So the mercy of God being infinite, it must be as sufficient for the pardon of all sin, as of one. If one of the least sins be not beyond the mercy of God, so neither are the greatest, or ten thousand of them. However, it must be acknowledged, that this alone doth not prove the doctrine. For though the mercy of God may be as sufficient for the pardon of great sins as others; yet there may be other obstacles, besides the want of mercy. The mercy of God may be sufficient, and yet the other attributes may oppose the dispensation of mercy in these cases.

2. *Therefore I observe, that the satisfaction of Christ is as sufficient for the removal of the greatest guilt, as the least:* 1 John 1.7: "The blood of Christ cleanseth from all sin." Acts 13:39: "By him all that believe are justified from all things from which ye could not be justified by the law of Moses." All the sins of those who truly come to God for mercy, let them be what they will, are satisfied for, if God be true who tells us so; and if they be satisfied for, surely it is not incredible, that God should be ready to pardon them. So that [since] Christ having fully satisfied for all sin, or having wrought out a satisfaction that is sufficient for all—it is now no way inconsistent with the glory of the divine attributes to pardon the greatest sins of those who in a right manner come unto him for it. God may now pardon the greatest sinners without any prejudice to the honor of his holiness. The holiness of God will not suffer him to give the least countenance to sin, but inclines him to give

proper testimonies of his hatred of it. But Christ having satisfied for sin, God can now love the sinner, and give no countenance at all to sin, however great a sinner he may have been. It was a sufficient testimony of God's abhorrence of sin, that he poured out his wrath on his own dear Son, when he took the guilt of it upon himself. Nothing can more show God's abhorrence of sin than this. If all mankind had been eternally damned, it would not have been so great a testimony of it.

God may, through Christ, pardon the greatest sinner without any prejudice to the honor of his majesty. The honor of the divine majesty indeed requires satisfaction; but the sufferings of Christ fully repair the injury. Let the contempt be ever so great, yet if so honorable a person as Christ undertakes to be a Mediator for the offender, and suffers so much for him, it fully repairs the injury done to the Majesty of heaven and earth. The sufferings of Christ fully satisfy justice. The justice of God, as the supreme Governor and Judge of the world, requires the punishment of sin. The supreme Judge must judge the world according to a rule of justice. God doth not show mercy as a judge, but as a sovereign; therefore his exercise of mercy as a sovereign, and his justice as a judge, must be made consistent one with another; and this is done by the sufferings of Christ, in which sin is punished fully, and justice answered. Rom. 3:25, 26:

> Whom God hath set forth to be a propitiation through faith in his blood, to declare his righteousness for the remission of sins that are past, through the forbearance of God; to declare, I say, at this time, his righteousness; that he might be just, and the justifier of him which believeth in Jesus.

The law is no impediment in the way of the pardon of the greatest sin, if men do but truly come to God for mercy: for Christ hath fulfilled the law, he hath borne the curse of it, in his sufferings; Gal. 3:13. "Christ hath redeemed us from the curse of the law, being made a curse for us; for it is written, "Cursed is every one that hangeth on a tree."

3. *Christ will not refuse to save the greatest sinners, who in a right manner come to God for mercy; for this is his work.* It is his business to be a Savior of sinners; it is the work upon which he came into the world; and therefore he will not object to it. He did not come to call the righteous, but sinners to repentance (Matt. 9:13). Sin is the very evil which he came into the world to remedy: therefore he will not object to any man that he is very sinful. The more sinful he is, the more need of Christ. The sinfulness of man was the reason of Christ's coming into the world; this is the very misery from which he came to deliver men. The more they have of it, the more need they have

of being delivered; "They that are whole need not a physician, but they that are sick," Matt. 9:12. The physician will not make it an objection against healing a man who applies to him, that he stands in great need of his help. If a physician of compassion comes among the sick and wounded, surely he will not refuse to heal those that stand in most need of healing, if he be able to heal them.

4. *Herein doth the glory of grace by the redemption of Christ much consist, viz. in its sufficiency for the pardon of the greatest sinners.* The whole contrivance of the way of salvation is for this end, to glorify the free grace of God. God had it on his heart from all eternity to glorify this attribute; and therefore it is, that the device of saving sinners by Christ was conceived. The greatness of divine grace appears very much in this, that God by Christ saves the greatest offenders. The greater the guilt of any sinner is, the more glorious and wonderful is the grace manifested in his pardon: Rom. 5:20. "Where sin abounded, grace did much more abound." The apostle, when telling how great a sinner he had been, takes notice of the abounding of grace in his pardon, of which his great guilt was the occasion: 1 Tim. 1:13. "Who was before a blasphemer, and a persecutor, and injurious. But I obtained mercy; and the grace of our Lord was exceeding abundant, with faith and love which is in Christ Jesus." The Redeemer is glorified, in that he proves sufficient to redeem those who are exceeding sinful, in that his blood proves sufficient to wash away the greatest guilt, in that he is able to save men to the uttermost, and in that he redeems even from the greatest misery. It is the honor of Christ to save the greatest sinners, when they come to him, as it is the honor of a physician that he cures the most desperate diseases or wounds. Therefore, no doubt, Christ will be willing to save the greatest sinners, if they come to him; for he will not be backward to glorify himself, and to commend the value and virtue of his own blood. Seeing he hath so laid out himself to redeem sinners, he will not be unwilling to show, that he is able to redeem to the uttermost.

5. *Pardon is as much offered and promised to the greatest sinners as any, if they will come aright to God for mercy.* The invitations of the gospel are always in universal terms: as, "Ho, every one that thirsteth"; "Come unto me, all ye that labor and are heavy laden"; and, "Whosoever will, let him come." And the voice of Wisdom is to men in general: Prov. 8:4. "Unto you, O men, I call, and my voice is to the sons of men." Not to moral men, or religious men, but to you, O men. So Christ promises, John 6:37: "Him that cometh to me, I will in no wise cast out." This is the direction of Christ to his

apostles, after his resurrection, Mark 16:15, 16. "Go ye into all the world, and preach the gospel to every creature: he that believeth, and is baptized, shall be saved." Which is agreeable to what the apostle saith, that "the gospel was preached to every creature which is under heaven," Col. 1:23.

Application

The proper use of this subject is, to encourage sinners whose consciences are burdened with a sense of guilt, immediately to go to God through Christ for mercy. If you go in the manner we have described, the arms of mercy are open to embrace you. You need not be at all the more fearful of coming because of your sins, let them be ever so black. If you had as much guilt lying on each of your souls as all the wicked men in the world, and all the damned souls in Hell; yet if you come to God for mercy, sensible of your own vileness, and seeking pardon only through the free mercy of God in Christ, you would not need to be afraid; the greatness of your sins would be no impediment to your pardon. Therefore, if your souls be burdened, and you are distressed for fear of Hell, you need not bear that burden and distress any longer. If you are but willing, you may freely come and unload yourselves, and cast all your burdens on Christ, and rest in him.

But here I shall speak to some *objections* which some awakened sinners may be ready to make against what I now exhort them to.

I. Some may be ready to object, "I have spent my youth and all the best of my life in sin, and I am afraid God will not accept of me, when I offer him only mine old age. "

To this I would answer,

1. *Hath God said any where, that he will not accept of old sinners who come to him?* God hath often made offers and promises in universal terms; and is there any such exception put in? Doth Christ say, "All that thirst, let them come to me and drink, except old sinners?" "Come to me, all ye that labor and are heavy laden, except old sinners, and I will give you rest?" "Him that cometh to me, I will in no wise cast out, if he be not an old sinner?" Did you ever read any such exception anywhere in the Bible? And why should you give way to exceptions which you make out of your own heads, or rather which the devil puts into your heads, and which have no foundation in the word of God? Indeed it is more rare that old sinners are willing to come,

than others; but if they do come, they are as readily accepted as any whatever.

2. When God accepts of young persons, it is not for the sake of the service which they are like to do him afterwards, or because youth is better worth accepting than old age. You seem entirely to mistake the matter, in thinking that God will not accept of you because you are old; as though he readily accepted of persons in their youth, because their youth is better worth his acceptance; whereas it is only for the sake of Jesus Christ, that God is willing to accept of any.

You say, your life is almost spent, and you are afraid that the best time for serving God is past; and that therefore God will not now accept of you; as if it were for the sake of the service which persons are like to do him, after they are converted, that he accepts of them. But a self-righteous spirit is at the bottom of such objections. Men cannot get off from the notion, that it is for some goodness or service of their own, either done or expected to be done, that God accepts of persons, and receives them into favor. Indeed they who deny God their youth, the best part of their lives, and spend it in the service of Satan, dreadfully sin and provoke God; and he very often leaves them to hardness of heart when they are grown old. But if they are willing to accept of Christ when old, he is as ready to receive them as any others; for in that matter God hath respect only to Christ and his worthiness.

II. But, says one,

I fear I have committed sins that are peculiar to reprobates. I have sinned against light, and strong convictions of conscience; I have sinned presumptuously; and have so resisted the strivings of the Spirit of God, that I am afraid I have committed such sins as none of God's elect ever commit. I cannot think that God will ever leave one whom he intends to save, to go on and commit sins against so much light and conviction, and with such horrid presumption.

Others may say,

I have had risings of heart against God; blasphemous thoughts, a spiteful and malicious spirit; and have abused mercy and the strivings of the Spirit, trampled upon the Savior, and my sins are such as are peculiar to those who are reprobated to eternal damnation.

To all this I would answer:

1. There is no sin peculiar to reprobates but the sin against the Holy Ghost. Do you read of any other in the word of God? And if you do not read of any there, what ground have you to think any such thing? What other rule have we, by which to judge of such matters, but the divine word? If we venture to go beyond that, we shall be miserably in the dark. When we pretend to go further in our determinations than the word of God, Satan takes us up, and leads us. It seems to you that such sins are peculiar to the reprobate, and such as God never forgives. But what reason can you give for it, if you have no word of God to reveal it? Is it because you cannot see how the mercy of God is sufficient to pardon, or the blood of Christ to cleanse from such presumptuous sins? If so, it is because you never yet saw how great the mercy of God is; you never saw the sufficiency of the blood of Christ, and you know not how far the virtue of it extends. Some elect persons have been guilty of all manner of sins, except the sin against the Holy Ghost; and unless you have been guilty of this, you have not been guilty of any that are peculiar to reprobates.

2. *Men may be less likely to* believe, *for sins which they have committed, not the less readily* pardoned *when they do believe.* It must be acknowledged that some sinners are in more danger of Hell than others. Though all are in great danger, some are less likely to be saved. Some are less likely ever to be converted and to come to Christ: but all who do come to him are alike readily accepted; and there is as much encouragement for one man to come to Christ as another. Such sins as you mention are indeed exceeding heinous and provoking to God, and do in an especial manner bring the soul into danger of damnation, and into danger of being given to final hardness of heart; and God more commonly gives men up to the judgment of final hardness for such sins, than for others. Yet they are not peculiar to reprobates; there is but one sin that is so, viz. that against the Holy Ghost. And notwithstanding the sins which you have committed, if you can find it in your hearts to come to Christ, and close with him, you will be accepted not at all the less readily because you have committed such sins.

Though God doth more rarely cause some sorts of sinners to come to Christ than others, it is not because his mercy or the redemption of Christ is not as sufficient for them as others, but because in wisdom he sees fit so to dispense his grace, for a restraint upon the wickedness of men; and because it is his will to give converting grace in the use of means, among which this is one, viz. to lead a moral and religious life, and agreeable to our light, and the convictions of our consciences. But when once any sinner is willing to come to Christ, mercy is as ready for him as for any. There is no consideration at all had of his sins; let him have been ever so sinful, his sins are not remembered; God doth not upbraid him with them.

III. "But had I not better stay till I shall have made myself better, before I presume to come to Christ?"

> I have been, and see myself to be very wicked now; but am in hopes of mending myself, and rendering myself at least not so wicked: then I shall have more courage to come to God for mercy.

In answer to this:

1. Consider how unreasonably you act. You are striving to set up yourselves for your own saviors; you are striving to get something of your own, on the account of which you may the more readily be accepted. So that by this it appears that you do not seek to be accepted only on Christ's account. And is not this to rob Christ of the glory of being your only Savior? Yet this is the way in which you are hoping to make Christ willing to save you.

2. You can never come to Christ at all, unless you first see that he will not accept of you the more readily for anything that you can do. You must first see, that it is utterly in vain for you to try to make yourselves better on any such account. You must see that you can never make yourselves any more worthy, or less unworthy, by anything which you can perform.

3. If ever you truly come to Christ, you must see that there is enough in him for your pardon, though you be no better than you are. If you see not the sufficiency of Christ to pardon you, without any righteousness of your own to recommend you, you never will come so as to be accepted of him. The way to be accepted is to come—not on any such encouragement, that now you have made yourselves better, and more worthy, or not so unworthy—but on the mere encouragement of Christ's worthiness, and God's mercy.

4. If ever you truly come to Christ, you must come to him to make you better. You must come as a patient comes to his physician, with his diseases or wounds to be cured. Spread all your wickedness before him, and do not plead your goodness; but plead your badness, and your necessity on that account: and say, as the psalmist in the text, not "Pardon mine iniquity, for it is not so great as it was," but, "Pardon mine iniquity, for it is great."

The Justice of God
in the Damnation of Sinners

Originally preached circa 1734–1735. "According to the estimate of Mr. Edwards, it was by far the most powerful and effectual of his discourses." (*Memoirs of Jonathan Edwards.*)

"That every mouth may be stopped."—Romans 3:19

The main subject of the doctrinal part of this epistle is the free grace of God in the salvation of men by Christ Jesus; especially as it appears in the doctrine of justification by faith alone. And the more clearly to evince this doctrine, and show the reason of it, the apostle, in the first place, establishes that point, that no flesh living can be justified by the deeds of the law. And to prove it, he is very large and particular in showing, that all mankind, not only the Gentiles, but Jews, are under sin, and so under the condemnation of the law; which is what he insists upon from the beginning of the epistle to this place.

He first begins with the Gentiles; and in the first chapter shows that they are under sin, by setting forth the exceeding corruptions and horrid wickedness that overspread the Gentile world: and then through the second chapter, and the former part of this third chapter, to the text and following verse, he shows the same of the Jews, that they also are in the same circumstances with the Gentiles in this regard. They had a high thought of themselves, because they were God's covenant people, and circumcised, and the children of Abraham. They despised the Gentiles as polluted, condemned, and accursed; but looked on themselves, on account of their external privileges, and ceremonial and moral righteousness, as a pure and holy people, and the children of God; as the apostle observes in the second chapter. It was therefore strange doctrine to them, that they also were unclean and guilty in God's sight, and under the condemnation and curse of the law. The apostle does therefore, on account of their strong prejudices against such doctrine, the more particularly insist upon it, and shows that they are no better than the Gentiles; and as in the 9th verse of this chapter, "What then? Are we better than they? No, in no wise; for we have before proved both Jews and Gentiles, that they are all under sin." And, to convince them of it, he then produces certain passages out of their own law, or the Old Testament, (to whose authority they pretend a great regard) from the ninth verse to our text. And it may be observed, that the apostle, first, cites certain passages to prove that all mankind is corrupt (verses 10–12).

> As it is written, there is none righteous, no, not one: There is none that understandeth, there is none that seeketh after God. They are all gone out of the way, they are together become unprofitable, there is none that doeth good, no, not one.

Secondly, the passages he cites next are to prove that not only all are corrupt, but each one wholly corrupt, as it were, all over unclean, from the crown of the head to the soles of his feet; and therefore several particular parts of the body are mentioned, the throat, the tongue, the lips, the mouth, the feet. Verses 13–15:

> Their throat is an open sepulcher; with their tongues they have used deceit; the poison of asps is under their lips; whose mouth is full of cursing and bitterness: their feet are swift to shed blood.

And, thirdly, he quotes other passages to show that each one is not only all over corrupt, but corrupt to a desperate degree, by affirming the most pernicious tendency of their wickedness; "Destruction and misery are in their ways." And then by denying all goodness or godliness in them; "And the way of peace have they not known: there is no fear of God before their eyes." And then, lest the Jews should think these passages of their law do not concern them, and only the Gentiles are intended in them, the apostle shows in the text, not only that they are not exempt, but that they especially must be understood: "Now we know that whatsoever things the law saith, it saith to them who are under the law." By those that are under the law is meant the Jews; and the Gentiles by those that are without law; as appears by the 12th verse of the preceding chapter. There is a special reason to understand the law, as speaking *to* and *of* them, to whom it was immediately given. And therefore the Jews would be unreasonable in exempting themselves. And if we examine the places of the Old Testament whence these passages are taken, we shall see plainly that special respect is had to the wickedness of the people of that nation, in every one of them. So that the law shuts all up in universal and desperate wickedness, that every mouth may be stopped; the mouths of the Jews, as well as of the Gentiles, notwithstanding all those privileges by which they were distinguished from the Gentiles.

The things that the law says, are sufficient to stop the mouths of all mankind, in two respects.

1. To stop them from boasting of their righteousness, as the Jews were wont to do; as the apostle observes in the 23rd verse of the preceding chapter. That the apostle has respect to stopping their mouths in this respect, appears by the 27th verse of the context, "Where is boasting then? It is excluded." The law stops our mouths from making any plea for life, or the favor of God, or any positive good, from our own righteousness.

2. To stop them from making any excuse for ourselves, or objection against the execution of the sentence of the law, or the infliction of the punishment that it threatens. That it is intended, appears by the words immediately following, "That all the world may become guilty before God." That is, that they may appear to be guilty, and stand convicted before God, and justly liable to the condemnation of his law, as guilty of death, according to the Jewish way of speaking.

And thus the apostle proves, that no flesh can be justified in God's sight by the deeds of the law; as he draws the conclusion in the following verse; and so prepares the way for establishing of the great doctrine of justification by faith alone, which he proceeds to do in the following part of the chapter, and of the epistle.

Doctrine

"It is just with God eternally to cast off and destroy sinners." For this is the punishment which the law condemns to. The truth of this doctrine may appear by the joint consideration of two things: viz. man's sinfulness, and God's sovereignty.

I. It appears from the consideration of man's sinfulness. And that whether we consider the infinitely evil nature of all sin, or how much sin men are guilty of.

1. *If we consider the infinite evil and heinousness of sin in general, it is not unjust in God to inflict what punishment is deserved; because the very notion of deserving any punishment is, that it may be justly inflicted.* A deserved punishment and a just punishment are the same thing. To say that one deserves such a punishment, and yet to say that he does not justly deserve it, is a contradiction; and if he justly deserves it, then it may be justly inflicted.

Every crime or fault deserves a greater or less punishment, in proportion as the crime itself is greater or less. If any fault deserves punishment, then so much the greater the fault, so much the greater is the punishment deserved. The faulty nature of anything is the formal ground and reason of its desert of punishment; and therefore the more anything hath of this nature, the more punishment it deserves. And therefore the terribleness of the degree of punishment, let it be never be so terrible, is no argument against the justice of it, if the proportion does but hold between the heinousness of the crime and the dreadfulness of the punishment; so that if there be any such thing as a fault infinitely heinous, it will follow that it is just to inflict a punishment for it that is infinitely dreadful.

A crime is more or less heinous, according as we are under greater or less obligations to the contrary. This is self-evident; because it is herein that the criminalness or faultiness of anything consists, that it is contrary to what we are obliged or bound to, or what ought to be in us. So the faultiness of one being hating another, is in proportion to his obligation to love him. The crime of one being despising and casting contempt on another, is proportionably more or less heinous, as he was under greater or less obligations to honor him. The fault of disobeying another, is greater or less, as anyone is under greater or less obligations to obey him. And therefore if there be any being that we are under infinite obligations to love, and honor, and obey, the contrary towards him must be infinitely faulty.

Our obligation to love, honor, and obey any being, is in proportion to his loveliness, honorableness, and authority; for that is the very meaning of the words. When we say anyone is very lovely, it is the same as to say, that he is one very much to be loved. Or if we say such a one is more honorable than another, the meaning of the words is, that he is one that we are more obliged to honor. If we say anyone has great authority over us, it is the same as to say, that he has great right to our subjection and obedience.

But God is a being infinitely lovely, because he hath infinite excellency and beauty. To have infinite excellency and beauty, is the same thing as to have infinite loveliness. He is a being of infinite greatness, majesty, and glory; and therefore he is infinitely honour able. He is infinitely exalted above the greatest potentates of the earth, and highest angels in heaven; and therefore he is infinitely more honour able than they. His authority over us is infinite; and the ground of his right to our obedience is infinitely strong; for he is infinitely worthy to be obeyed himself, and we have an absolute, universal, and infinite dependence upon him.

So that sin against God, being a violation of infinite obligations, must be a crime infinitely heinous, and so deserving of infinite punishment. Nothing is more agreeable to the common sense of mankind, than that sins committed against anyone, must be proportionably heinous to the dignity of the being offended and abused; as it is also agreeable to the word of God. 1 Samuel 2:25: "If one man sin against another, the judge shall judge him;" (i.e. shall judge him, and inflict a finite punishment, such as finite judges can inflict;) "but if a man sin against the Lord, who shall entreat for him?" This was the aggravation of sin that made Joseph afraid of it. Genesis 39:9: "How shall I commit this great wickedness, and sin against God?" This was the aggravation of David's sin, in comparison of which he esteemed all others as nothing, because they were infinitely exceeded by it. Psalm 51:4: "Against thee, thee only have I sinned." The eternity of the punishment of ungodly men renders it infinite: and it renders it no more than infinite; and therefore renders no more than proportionable to the heinousness of what they are guilty of.

If there be any evil or faultiness in sin against God, there is certainly infinite evil: for if it be any fault at all, it has an infinite aggravation, viz. that it is against an infinite object. If it be ever so small upon other accounts, yet if it be anything, it has one infinite dimension; and so is an infinite evil. Which may be illustrated by this: if we suppose a thing to have infinite length, but no breadth and thickness, (a mere mathematical line,) it is nothing: but if it have any breadth and thickness, though never so small, and infinite length, the quantity of it is infinite; it exceeds the quantity of anything, however broad, thick, and long, wherein these dimensions are all finite.

So that the objections made against the infinite punishment of sin, from the necessity, or rather previous certainty, of the futurition [future state of being] of sin, arising from the unavoidable original corruption of nature, if they argue anything, argue against any faultiness at all: for if this necessity or certainty leaves any evil at all in sin, that fault must be infinite by reason of the infinite object.

But every such objector as would argue from hence, that there is no fault at all in sin, confutes [confounds] himself, and shows his own insincerity in his objection. For at the same time that he objects that men's acts are necessary, and that this kind of necessity is inconsistent with faultiness in the act, his own practice shows that he does not believe what he objects to be true: otherwise why does he at all blame men? Or why are such persons at all displeased with men, for abusive, injurious, and ungrateful acts towards them? Whatever they pretend, by this they show that indeed they do believe that there is no necessity in men's acts that is inconsistent with blame. And if their objection be this, that this previous certainty is by God's own ordering, and that where God orders an antecedent certainty of acts, he transfers all the fault from the actor on himself; their practice shows, that at the same time they do not believe this, but fully believe the contrary: for when they are abused by men, they are displeased with men, and not with God only.

The light of nature teaches all mankind, that when an injury is voluntary, it is faulty, without any consideration of what there might be previously to determine the futurition of that evil act of the will. And it really teaches this as much to those that object and cavil most as to others; as their universal practice shows. By which it appears, that such objections are insincere and perverse. Men will mention others' corrupt nature when they are injured, as a thing that aggravates their crime, and that wherein their faultiness partly consists. How common is it for persons, when they look on themselves greatly injured by another, to inveigh against him, and aggravate his baseness, by saying, "He is a man of a most perverse spirit: he is naturally of a selfish, niggardly, or proud and haughty temper: he is one of a base and vile disposition." And yet men's natural and corrupt dispositions are mentioned as an excuse for them, with respect to their sins against God, as if they rendered them blameless.

2. That it is just with God eternally to cast off wicked men, [it] may more abundantly appear [just], if we consider how much sin they are guilty of. From what has been already said, it appears, that if men were guilty of sin but in one particular, that is sufficient ground of their eternal rejection and condemnation. If they are sinners, that is enough. Merely this, might be sufficient to keep them from ever lifting up their heads, and cause them to smite on their breasts, with the publican that cried, "God be merciful to me, a sinner." But sinful men are full of sin; full of principles and acts of sin: their guilt is like great mountains, heaped one upon another, till the pile is grown up to heaven. They are totally corrupt, in every part, in all their faculties, and all the principles of their nature, their understandings, and wills; and in all their dispositions and affections. Their heads, their hearts, are totally depraved; all the members of their bodies are only instruments of sin; and all their senses, seeing, hearing, tasting, etc. are only inlets and outlets of sin, channels of corruption.

There is nothing but sin, no good at all. Romans. 7:18: "In me, that is, in my flesh, dwells no good thing." There is all manner of wickedness. There are the seeds of the greatest and blackest crimes. There are principles of all sorts of wickedness against men; and there is all wickedness against God. There is pride; there is enmity; there is contempt; there is quarreling; there is atheism; there is blasphemy. There are these things in exceeding strength; the heart is under the power of them, is sold under sin, and is a perfect slave to it. There is hard-heartedness, hardness greater than that of a rock, or an adamant-stone. There is obstinacy and perverseness, incorrigibleness and inflexibleness in sin, that will not be overcome by threatenings or promises, by awakenings or encouragements, by judgments or mercies, neither by that which is terrifying nor that which is winning. The very blood of God our Savior will not win the heart of a wicked man.

And there are actual wickednesses without number or measure. There are breaches of every command, in thought, word, and deed: a life full of sin; days and nights filled up with sin; mercies abused and frowns despised; mercy and justice, and all the divine perfections, trampled on; and the honor of each person in the Trinity trod in the dirt. Now if one sinful word or thought has so much evil in it, as to deserve eternal destruction, how do they deserve to be eternally cast off and destroyed, that are guilty of so much sin!

II. If with man's sinfulness, we consider God's sovereignty, it may serve further to clear God's justice in the eternal rejection and condemnation of sinners, from men's cavils and objections.

I shall not now pretend to determine precisely, what things are, and what things are not, proper acts and exercises of God's holy sovereignty; but only, that God's sovereignty extends to the following things.

1. That such is God's sovereign power and right, that he is originally under no obligation to keep men from sinning; but may in his providence permit and leave them to sin. He was not obliged to keep either angels or men from falling. It is unreasonable to suppose, that God should be obliged, if he makes a reasonable creature capable of knowing his will, and receiving a law from him, and being subject to his moral government; at the same time to make it impossible for him to sin, or break his law. For if God be obliged to this, it destroys all use of any commands, laws, promises, or threatenings, and the very notion of any moral government of God over those reasonable creatures. For to what purpose would it be, for God to give such and such laws, and declare his holy will to a creature, and annex promises and threatenings to move him to his duty, and make him careful to perform it, if the creature at the same time has this to think of, that God is obliged to make it impossible for him to break his laws? How can God's threatenings move to care or watchfulness, when, at the same time, God is obliged to render it impossible that he should be exposed to the threatenings? Or, to what purpose is it for God to give a law at all? For according to this supposition, it is God, and not the creature, that is under the law. It is the lawgiver's care, and not the subject's, to see that his law is obeyed; and this care is what the lawgiver is absolutely obliged to! If God be obliged never to permit a creature to fall, there is an end of all divine laws, or government, or authority of God over the creature; there can be no manner of use of these things.

God may permit sin, though the being of sin will certainly ensue on that permission: and so, by permission, he may dispose and order the event. If there were any such thing as chance, or mere contingence, and the very notion of it did not carry a gross absurdity, (as might easily be shown that it does,) it would have been very unfit that God should have left it to mere chance, whether man should fall or no. For chance, if there should be any such thing, is undesigning and blind. And certainly it is more fit that an event of so great importance, and that is attended with such an infinite train of great consequences, should be disposed and ordered by infinite wisdom, than that it should be left to blind chance.

If it be said, that God need not have interposed to render it impossible for man to sin, and yet not leave it to mere contingence or blind chance neither; but might have left it with man's free will, to determine whether to sin or no: I answer, if God did leave it to man's free will, without any sort of disposal, or ordering [or rather, adequate cause] in the case, whence it should be previously certain how that free will should determine, then still that first determination of the will must be merely contingent or by chance. It could not have any antecedent act of the will to determine it; for I speak now of the very first act of motion of the will, respecting the affair that may be looked upon as the prime ground and highest source of the event. To suppose this to be determined by a foregoing act is a contradiction. God's disposing this determination of the will by his permission, does not at all infringe the liberty of the creature: it is in no respect any more inconsistent with liberty, than mere chance or contingence. For if the determination of the will be from blind, undesigning chance, it is no more from the agent himself, or from the will itself, than if we suppose, in the case, a wise, divine disposal by permission.

2. *It was fit that it should be at the ordering of the divine wisdom and good pleasure, whether every particular man should stand for himself, or whether the first father of mankind should be appointed as the moral and federal head and representative of the rest.* If God has not liberty in this matter to determine either of these two as he pleases, it must be because determining that the first father of men should represent the rest, and not that every one should stand for himself, is injurious to mankind. For if it be not injurious, how is it unjust? But it is not injurious to mankind; for there is nothing in the nature of the case itself, that makes it better that each man should stand for himself, than that all should be represented by their common father; as the least reflection or consideration will convince anyone. And if there be nothing in the nature of the thing that makes the former better for mankind than the latter, then it will follow, that they are not hurt in God's choosing and appointing the latter, rather than the former; or, which is the same thing, that it is not injurious to mankind.

3. *When men are fallen, and become sinful, God by his sovereignty has a right to determine about their redemption as he pleases.* He has a right to determine whether he will redeem any or not. He might, if he had pleased, have left all to perish, or might have redeemed all. Or, he may redeem some, and leave others; and if he doth so, he may take whom he pleases, and leave whom he pleases. To suppose that all have forfeited his favor, and deserved to perish, and to suppose that he may not leave any one individual of them to perish, implies a contradiction; because it supposes that such a one has a claim to God's favor, and is not justly liable to perish; which is contrary to the supposition.

It is meet that God should order all these things according to his own pleasure. By reason of his greatness and glory, by which he is infinitely above all, he is worthy to be sovereign, and that his pleasure should in all things take place. He is worthy that he should make himself his end, and that he should make nothing but his own wisdom his rule in pursuing that end, without asking leave or counsel of any, and without giving account of any of his matters. It is fit that he who is absolutely perfect, and infinitely wise, and the Fountain of all wisdom, should determine every thing [that he effects] by his own will, even things of the greatest importance. It is meet that he should be thus sovereign, because he is the first being, the eternal being, whence all other beings are. He is the Creator of all things; and all are absolutely and universally dependent on him; and therefore it is meet that he should act as the sovereign possessor of heaven and earth.

Application

In the improvement of this doctrine, I would chiefly direct myself to sinners who are afraid of damnation, in a use of conviction. This may be matter of conviction to you, that it would be just and righteous with God eternally to reject and destroy you. This is what you are in danger of. You who are a Christless sinner are a poor condemned creature: God's wrath still abides upon you; and the sentence of condemnation lies upon you. You are in God's hands, and it is uncertain what he will do with you. You are afraid what will become of you. You are afraid that it will be your portion to suffer eternal burnings; and your fears are not without grounds; you have reason to tremble every moment. But be you never so much afraid of it, let eternal damnation be never so dreadful, yet it is just. God may nevertheless do it, and be righteous, and holy, and glorious. Though eternal damnation be what you cannot bear, and how much soever your heart shrinks at the thought of it, yet God's justice may be glorious in it. The dreadfulness of the thing on your part, and the greatness of your dread of it, do not render it the less righteous on God's part. If you think otherwise, it is a sign that you do not see yourself, that you are not sensible what sin is, nor how much of it you have been guilty of. Therefore for your conviction, be directed:

1. *To look over your past life: inquire at the mouth of conscience, and hear what that has to testify concerning it.* Consider what you are, what light you have had, and what means you have lived under: and yet how you have behaved yourself! What have those many days and nights you have lived been filled up with? How have those years that have rolled over your heads, one after another, been spent? What has the sun shone upon you for, from day to day, while you have improved his light to serve Satan by it? What has

God kept your breath in your nostrils for, and given you meat and drink, that you have spent your life and strength, supported by them, in opposing God, and rebellion against him?

How many sorts of wickedness have you not been guilty of! How manifold have been the abominations of your life! What profaneness and contempt of God has been exercised by you! How little regard have you had to the Scriptures, to the word preached, to sabbaths, and sacraments! How profanely have you talked, many of you, about those things that are holy! After what manner have many of you kept God's holy day, not regarding the holiness of the time, not caring what you thought of in it! Yea, you have not only spent the time in worldly, vain, and unprofitable thoughts, but in immoral thoughts; pleasing yourself with the reflection on past acts of wickedness, and in contriving new acts. Have not you spent much holy time in gratifying your lusts in your imaginations; yea, not only holy time, but the very time of God's public worship, when you have appeared in God's more immediate presence? How have you not only attended to the worship, but have in the mean time been feasting your lusts, and wallowing yourself in abominable uncleanness! How many sabbaths have you spent, one after another, in a most wretched manner! Some of you not only in worldly and wicked thoughts, but also a very wicked outward behavior! When you on sabbath-days have got along with your wicked companions, how has holy time been treated among you! What kind of conversation has there been! Yea, how have some of you, by a very indecent carriage, openly dishonored and cast contempt on the sacred services of God's house, and holy day! And what you have done some of you alone, what wicked practices there have been in secret, even in holy time, God and your own consciences know.

And how have you behaved yourself in the time of family prayer! And what a trade have many of you made of absenting yourselves from the worship of the families you belong to, for the sake of vain company! And how have you continued in the neglect of secret prayer! Therein wilfully living in a known sin, going abreast against as plain a command as any in the Bible! Have you not been one that has cast off fear, and restrained prayer before God?

What wicked carriage have some of you been guilty of towards your parents! How far have you been from paying that honor to them which God has required! Have you not even harbored ill-will and malice towards them? And when they have displeased you, have wished evil to them? Yea, and shown your vile spirit in your behavior? And it is well if you have not mocked them behind their backs; and, like the cursed Ham and Canaan, as it were, derided your parents' nakedness instead of covering it, and hiding your eyes from it. Have not some of you often disobeyed your parents, yea, and refused to be subject to them? Is it not a wonder of mercy and forbearance, that the proverb has not before now been accomplished on you: Proverbs 30:17: "The eye that mocketh at his father, and refuseth to obey his mother, the ravens of the valley shall pick it out, and the young eagles shall eat it."

What revenge and malice have you been guilty of towards your neighbors! How have you indulged this spirit of the devil, hating others, and wishing evil to them, rejoicing when evil befell them, and grieving at others' prosperity, and lived in such a way for a long time! Have not some of you allowed a passionate furious spirit, and behaved yourselves in your anger more like wild beasts than like Christians?

What covetousness has been in many of you! Such has been your inordinate love of the world, and care about the things of it, that it has taken up your heart; you have allowed no room for God and religion; you have minded the world more than your eternal salvation. For the vanities of the world you have neglected reading, praying and meditation; for the things of the world, you have broken the sabbath: for the world you have spent a great deal of your time in quarreling. For the world you have envied and hated your neighbor; for the world you have cast God, and Christ, and heaven, behind your back; for the world you have sold your own soul. You have as it were drowned your soul in worldly cares and desires; you have been a mere earth-worm, that is never in its element but when groveling and buried in the earth.

How much of a spirit of pride has appeared in you, which is in a peculiar manner the spirit and condemnation of the devil! How have some of you vaunted yourselves in your apparel! Others in their riches! Others in their knowledge and abilities! How has it galled you to see others above you! How much has it gone against the grain for you to give others their due honor! And how have you shown your pride by setting up your wills and in opposing others, and stirring up and promoting division, and a party spirit in public affairs.

How sensual have you been! Are there not some here that have debased themselves below the dignity of human nature, by wallowing in sensual filthiness, as swine in the mire, or as filthy vermin feeding with delight on rotten carrion? What intemperance have some of you been guilty of! How much of your precious time have you spent at the tavern, and in drinking companies, when you ought to have been at home seeking God and your salvation in your families and closets!

And what abominable lasciviousness have some of you been guilty of! How have you indulged yourself from day to day, and from night to night, in all manner of unclean imaginations! Has not your soul been filled with them, till it has become a hold of foul spirits, and a cage of every unclean and hateful bird? What foul-mouthed persons have some of you been, often in lewd and lascivious talk and unclean songs, wherein were things not fit to be spoken! And such company, where such conversation has been carried on, has been your delight. And with what unclean acts and practices have you defiled yourself! God and your own consciences know what abominable lasciviousness you have practiced in things not fit to be named, when you have been alone; when you ought to have been reading, or meditating, or on your knees before God in secret prayer. And how have you corrupted others, as well as polluted yourselves! What vile uncleanness have you practiced in company! What abominations have you been guilty of in the dark! Such as the apostle doubtless had respect to in Ephesians 5:12: "For it is a shame even to speak of those things that are done of them in secret." Some of you have corrupted others, and done what in you lay to undo their souls, (if you have not actually done it;) and by your vile practices and example have made room for Satan, invited his presence, and established his interest, in the town where you have lived.

What lying have some of you been guilty of, especially in your childhood! And have not your heart and lips often disagreed since you came to riper years? What fraud, and deceit, and unfaithfulness, have many of you practiced in your own dealings with your neighbors, of which your own heart is conscious, if you have not been noted by others.

And how have some of you behaved yourselves in your family relations! How have you neglected your children's souls! And not only so, but have corrupted their minds by your bad examples; and instead of training them up in the nurture and admonition of the Lord, have rather brought them up in the devil's service!

How have some of you attended that sacred ordinance of the Lord's supper without any manner of serious preparation, and in a careless, slighty frame of spirits, and chiefly to comply with custom! Have you not ventured to put the sacred symbols of the body and blood of Christ into your mouth, while at the same time you lived in ways of known sins, and intended no other than still to go on in the same wicked practices? And, it may be, have sat at the Lord's table with rancor in your heart against some of your brethren that you have sat there with. You have come even to that holy feast of love among God's children, with the leaven of malice and envy in your heart; and so have eaten and drank judgment to yourself.

What stupidity and sottishness has attended your course of wickedness: which has appeared in your obstinacy under awakening dispensations of God's word and providence. And how have some of you backslidden after you have set out in religion, and quenched God's Spirit after he had been striving with you! And what unsteadiness, and slothfulness, and long misimprovement of God's strivings with you, have you been chargeable with!

Now, can you think when you have thus behaved yourself, that God is obliged to show you mercy? Are you not after all this ashamed to talk of its being hard with God to cast you off? Does it become one who has lived such a life to open his mouth to excuse himself, to object against God's justice in his condemnation, or to complain of it as hard in God not to give him converting and pardoning grace, and make him his child, and bestow on him eternal life? Or to talk of his duties and great pains in religion, as if such performances were worthy to be accepted, and to draw God's heart to such a creature? If this has been your manner, does it not show how little you have considered yourself, and how little a sense you have had of your own sinfulness?

2. Be directed to consider, if God should eternally reject and destroy you, what an agreeableness and exact mutual answerableness there would be between God so dealing with you, and your spirit and behavior. There would not only be an equality, but a similitude. God declares, that his dealings with men shall be suitable to their disposition and practice. Psalm 18:25, 26:

> With the merciful man, thou wilt show thyself merciful; with an upright man, thou wilt show thyself upright; with the pure, thou wilt show thyself pure; and with the froward, thou wilt show thyself froward.

How much soever you dread damnation, and are affrighted and concerned at the thoughts of it; yet if God should indeed eternally damn you, you would be met with but in your own way; you would be dealt with exactly according to your own dealing. Surely it is but fair that you should be made to buy in the same measure in which you sell.

Here I would particularly show:

> 1. That if God should eternally destroy you, it would be agreeable to your treatment of God.

> 2. That it would be agreeable to your treatment of Jesus Christ.

3. That it would be agreeable to your behavior towards your neighbors.

4. That it would be according to your own foolish behavior towards yourself.

I. If God should forever cast you off, it would be exactly agreeable to your treatment of him. That you may be sensible of this, consider,

1. *You never have exercised the least degree of love to God; and therefore it would be agreeable to your treatment of him, if he should never express any love to you.* When God converts and saves a sinner, it is a wonderful and unspeakable manifestation of divine love. When a poor lost soul is brought home to Christ, and has all his sins forgiven him, and is made a child of God, it will take up a whole eternity to express and declare the greatness of that love. And why should God be obliged to express such wonderful love to you, who never exercised the least degree of love to him in all your life? You never have loved God, who is infinitely glorious and lovely; and why then is God under obligation to love you, who are all over deformed and loathsome as a filthy worm, or rather a hateful viper? You have no benevolence in your heart towards God; you never rejoiced in God's happiness; if he had been miserable, and that had been possible, you would have liked it as well as if he were happy; you would not have cared how miserable he was, nor mourned for it, any more than you now do for the devil's being miserable. And why then should God be looked upon as obliged to take so much care for your happiness, as to do such great things for it, as he doth for those that are saved? Or why should God be called hard, in case he should not be careful to save you from misery? You care not what becomes of God's glory; you are not distressed how much soever his honor seems to suffer in the world: and why should God care any more for your welfare?

Has it not been so, that if you could but promote your private interest, and gratify your own lusts, you cared not how much the glory of God suffered? And why may not God advance his own glory in the ruin of your welfare, not caring how much your interest suffers by it? You never so much as stirred one step, sincerely making the glory of God your end, or acting from real respect to him: and why then is it hard if God doth not do such great things for you, as the changing of your nature, raising you from spiritual death to life, conquering the powers of darkness for you, translating you out of the kingdom of darkness into the kingdom of his dear Son, delivering you from eternal misery, and bestowing upon you eternal glory? You were not willing to deny yourself for God; you never cared to put yourself out of your way for Christ; whenever anything cross or difficult came in your way, that the glory of God was concerned in, it has been your manner to shun it, and excuse yourself from it. You did not care to hurt yourself for Christ, whom you did not see worthy of it; and why then must it be looked upon as a hard and cruel thing, if Christ has not been pleased to spill his blood and be tormented to death for such a sinner.

2. *You have slighted God; and why then may not God justly slight you?* When sinners are sensible in some measure of their misery, they are ready to think it hard that God will take no notice of them; that he will see them in such a lamentable distressed condition, beholding their burdens and tears, and seem to slight it, and manifest no pity to them. Their souls, they think, are precious: it would be a dreadful thing if they should perish, and burn in Hell for ever. They do not see through it, that God should make so light of their salvation. But then, ought they not to consider, that as their souls are precious, so is God's honor precious? The honor of the infinite God, the great King of heaven and earth, is a thing of as great importance, (and surely may justly be so esteemed by God,) as the happiness of you, a poor little worm. But yet you have slighted that honor of God, and valued it no more than the dirt under your feet. You have been told that such and such things were contrary to the will of a holy God, and against his honor; but you cared not for that. God called upon you, and exhorted you to be more tender of his honor; but you went on without regarding him. Thus have you slighted God! And yet, is it hard that God should slight you? Are you more honourable than God, that he must be obliged to make much of you, how light soever you make of him and his glory?

And you have not only slighted God in time past, but you slight him still. You indeed now make a pretense and show of honoring him in your prayers, and attendance on other external duties, and by sober countenance, and seeming devoutness in your words and behavior; but it if all mere dissembling. That downcast look and seeming reverence, is not from any honor you have to God in your heart, though you would have God take it so. You who have not believed in Christ, have not the least jot of honor to God; that show of it is merely forced, and what you are driven to by fear, like those mentioned in Psalm 66:3: "Through the greatness of thy power shall thine enemies submit themselves to thee." In the original it is, "shall lie unto thee;" that is, yield feigned submission, and dissemble respect and honor to thee. There is a rod held over you that makes you seem to pay such respect to God. This religion and devotion, even the very appearance of it, would soon be gone, and all vanish away, if that were removed. Sometimes it may be you weep in your prayers, and in your hearing sermons, and hope God will take notice of it, and take it for some honor; but he sees it to be all hypocrisy. You weep for yourself; you are afraid of Hell; and do you think that is worthy of God to take much notice of you, because you can cry when you are in danger of being damned; when at the same time you indeed care nothing for God's honor.

Seeing you thus disregard so great a God, is it a heinous thing for God to slight you, a little, wretched, despicable creature; a worm, a mere nothing, and less than nothing; a vile insect, that has risen up in contempt against the Majesty of heaven and earth?

3. *Why should God be looked upon as obliged to bestow salvation upon you, when you have been so ungrateful for the mercies he has bestowed upon you already?* God has tried you with a great deal of kindness, and he never has sincerely been thanked by you for any of it. God has watched over you, and preserved you, and provided for you, and followed you with mercy all your days; and yet you have continued sinning against him. He has given you food and raiment, but you have improved both in the service of sin. He has preserved you while you slept; but when you arose, it was to return to the old trade of sinning. God, notwithstanding this ingratitude, has still continued his mercy; but his kindness has never won your heart, or brought you to a more grateful behavior towards him. It may be you have received many remarkable mercies, recoveries from sickness, or preservations of your life when exposed by accidents, when if you had died, you would have gone directly to Hell; but you never had any true thankfulness for any of these mercies. God has kept you out of Hell, and continued your day of grace, and the offers of salvation, so long a time; while you did not regard your own salvation so much as in secret to ask God for it. And now God has greatly added to his mercy to you, by giving you the strivings of his Spirit, whereby a most precious opportunity for your salvation is in your hands. But what thanks has God received for it? What kind of returns have you made for all this kindness? As God has multiplied mercies, so have you multiplied provocations.

And yet now are you ready to quarrel for mercy, and to find fault with God, not only that he does not bestow more mercy, but to contend with him, because he does not bestow infinite mercy upon you, heaven with all it contains, and even himself, for your eternal portion. What ideas have you of yourself, that you think God is obliged to do so much for you, though you treat him ever so ungratefully for his kindness wherewith you have been followed all the days of your life?

4. *You have voluntarily chosen to be with Satan in his enmity and opposition to God; how justly therefore might you be with him in his punishment!* You did not choose to be on God's side, but rather chose to side with the devil, and have obstinately continued in it, against God's often repeated calls and counsels. You have chosen rather to hearken to Satan than to God, and would be with him in his work. You have given yourself up to him, to be subject to his power and government, in opposition to God; how justly therefore may God also give you up to him, and leave you in his power, to accomplish your ruin! Seeing you have yielded yourself to his will, to do as he would have you, surely God may leave you in his hands to execute his will upon you. If men will be with God's enemy, and on his side, why is God obliged to redeem them out of his hands, when they have done his work? Doubtless you would be glad to serve the devil, and be God's enemy while you live, and then to have God your friend, and deliver you from the devil, when you come to die. But will God be unjust if he deals otherwise by you? No, surely! It will be altogether and perfectly just, that you should have your portion with him with whom you have chosen to work; and that you should be in his possession to whose dominion you have yielded yourself; and if you cry to God for deliverance, he may most justly give you that answer. Judges 10:14. "Go to the gods which you have chosen."

5. *Consider how often you have refused to hear God's calls to you, and how just it would therefore be, if he should refuse to hear you when you call upon him.* You are ready, it may be, to complain that you have often prayed, and earnestly begged of God to show you mercy, and yet have no answer of prayer: One says, I have been constant in prayer for so many years, and God has not heard me. Another says, I have done what I can; I have prayed as earnestly as I am able; I do not see how I can do more; and it will seem hard if after all I am denied. But do you consider how often God has called, and you have denied him? God has called earnestly, and for a long time; he has called and called again in his word, and in his providence, and you have refused. You was not uneasy for fear you should not show regard enough to his calls. You let him call as loud and as long as he would; for your part, you had no leisure to attend to what he said; you had other business to mind; you had these and those lusts to gratify and please, and worldly concerns to attend; you could not afford to stand considering of what God had to say to you. When the ministers of Christ have

stood and pleaded with you, in his name, sabbath after sabbath, and have even spent their strength in it, how little was you moved! It did not alter you, but you went on still as you used to do; when you went away, you returned again to your sins, to your lasciviousness, to your vain mirth, to your covetousness, to your intemperance, and that has been the language of your heart and practice, Exodus 5:2. "Who is the Lord, that I should obey his voice?" Was it no crime for you to refuse to hear when God called? And yet is it now very hard that God does not hear your earnest calls, and that though your calling on God be not from any respect to him, but merely from self-love? The devil would beg as earnestly as you, if he had any hope to get salvation by it, and a thousand times as earnestly, and yet be as much of a devil as he is now. Are your calls more worthy to be heard than God's? Or is God more obliged to regard what you say to him, than you to regard his commands, counsels, and invitations to you? What can be more justice than this. Proverbs 1:24, etc.:

> Because I have called, and ye refused, I have stretched out my hand, and no man regarded; but ye have set at nought all my counsel, and would none of my reproof: I will also laugh at your calamity, I will mock when your fear cometh; when your fear cometh as desolation, and your destruction cometh as a whirlwind; when distress and anguish cometh upon you. Then shall they call upon me, but I will not answer; they shall seek me early, but they shall not find me.

6. *Have you not taken encouragement to sin against God, on that very presumption, that God would show you mercy when you sought it?* And may not God justly refuse you that mercy that you have so presumed upon? You have flattered yourself, that though you did so, yet God would show you mercy when you cried earnestly to him for it: how righteous therefore would it be in God, to disappoint such a wicked presumption! It was upon that very hope that you dared to affront the majesty of heaven so dreadfully as you have done; and can you now be so sottish as to think that God is obliged not to frustrate that hope?

When a sinner takes encouragement to neglect secret prayer which God has commanded, to gratify his lusts, to live a carnal vain life, to thwart God, to run upon him, and contemn him to his face, thinking with himself, "If I do so, God would not damn me; he is a merciful God, and therefore when I seek his mercy he will bestow it upon me;" must God be accounted hard because he will not do according to such a sinner's presumption?

Cannot he be excused from showing such a sinner mercy when he is pleased to seek it, without incurring the charge of being unjust; if this be the case, God has no liberty to vindicate his own honor and majesty; but must lay himself open to all manner of affronts, and yield himself up to the abuse of vile men, though they disobey, despise, and dishonor him, as much as they will; and when they have done, his mercy and pardoning grace must not be in his own power and at his own disposal, but he must be obliged to dispense it at their call. He must take these bold and vile contemners of his majesty, when it suits them to ask it, and must forgive all their sins, and not only so, but must adopt them into his family, and make them his children, and bestow eternal glory upon them. What mean, low, and strange thoughts have such men of God, who think thus of him! Consider, that you have injured God the more, and have been the worse enemy to him, for his being a merciful God. So have you treated that attribute of God's mercy! How just is it therefore that you never should have any benefit of that attribute!

There is something peculiarly heinous in sinning against the mercy of God more than other attributes. There is such base and horrid ingratitude, in being the worse to God because he is a being of infinite goodness and grace, that it above all things renders wickedness vile and detestable. This ought to win us, and engage us to serve God better; but instead of that, to sin against him the more, has something inexpressibly bad in it, and does in a peculiar manner enhance guilt, and incense wrath; as seems to be intimated. Romans 2:4, 5:

> Or despisest thou the riches of his goodness, and forbearance, and long-suffering; not knowing that the goodness of God leadeth thee to repentance? But after thy hardness and impenitent heart, treasurest up unto thyself wrath against the day of wrath and revelation of the righteous judgment of God.

The greater the mercy of God is, the more should you be engaged to love him, and live to his glory. But it has been contrariwise with you; the consideration of the mercies of God being so exceeding great, is the thing wherewith you have encouraged yourself in sin. You have heard that the mercy of God was without bounds, that it was sufficient to pardon the greatest sinner, and you have upon that very account ventured to be a very great sinner. Though it was very offensive to God, though you heard that God infinitely hated sin, and that such practices as you went on in were exceeding contrary to his nature, will, and glory, yet that did not make you uneasy; you heard that he was a very merciful God, and had grace enough to pardon you, and so cared not how offensive your sins were to him. How long have some of you gone on in sin, and what great sins have some of you been guilty of, on that presumption! Your own conscience can give testimony to it, that this has made you refuse God's calls, and has made you regardless of his repeated commands. Now, how righteous would it be if God should swear in his wrath, that you should never be the better for his being infinitely merciful!

Your ingratitude has been the greater, that you have not only abused the attribute of God's mercy, taking encouragement from it to continue in sin, but you have also presumed that God would exercise infinite mercy to you in particular; which consideration should have especially endeared God to you. You have taken encouragement to sin the more, from that consideration, that Christ came into the would and died to save sinners; such thanks has Christ had from you, for enduring such a tormenting death for his enemies! Now, how justly might God refuse that you should ever be the better for his Son's laying down his life! It was because of these things that you put off seeking salvation. You would take the pleasures of sin still longer, hardening yourself because mercy was infinite, and it would not be too late, if you sought it afterwards; now, how justly may God disappoint you in this, and so order it that it shall be too late!

7. *How have some of you risen up against God, and in the frame of your minds opposed him in his sovereign dispensations!* And how justly upon that account might God oppose you, and set himself against you! You never yet would submit to God; never willingly comply, that God should have dominion over the world, and that he should govern it for his own glory, according to his own wisdom. You, a poor worm, a potsherd, a broken piece of an earthen vessel, have dared to find fault and quarrel with God. Isaiah 45:9:

> Woe to him that striveth with his Maker. Let the potsherd strive with the potsherds of the earth: shall the clay say to him that fashioned it, "What makest thou?"

But yet you have ventured to do it. Romans 9:20: "Who art thou, O man, that repliest against God?" But yet you have thought you was big enough; you have taken upon you to call God to an account, why he does thus and thus; you have said to Jehovah, "What dost thou?"

If you have been restrained by fear from openly venting your opposition and enmity of heart against God's government, yet it has been in you; you have not been quiet in the frame of your mind; you have had the heart of a viper within, and have been ready to spit your venom at God. It is well if sometimes you have not actually done it, by tolerating blasphemous thoughts and malignant risings of heart against him; yea, and the frame of your heart in some measure appeared in impatient and fretful behavior. Now, seeing you have thus opposed God, how just is it that God should oppose you! Or is it because you are so much better, and so much greater than God, that it is a crime for him to make that opposition against you which you make against him? Do you think that the liberty of making opposition is your exclusive prerogative, so that you may be an enemy to God, but God must by no means be an enemy to you, but must be looked upon under obligation nevertheless to help you, and save you by his blood, and bestow his best blessings upon you?

Consider how in the frame of your mind you have thwarted God in those very exercises of mercy towards others that you are seeking for yourself. God exercising his infinite grace towards your neighbors, has put you into an ill frame, and it may be, set you into a tumult of mind. How justly therefore may God refuse ever to exercise that mercy towards you! Have you not thus opposed God showing mercy to others, even at the very time when you pretended to be earnest with God for pity and help for yourself? Yea, and while you was endeavoring to get something wherewith to recommend yourself to God? And will you look to God still with a challenge of mercy, and contend with him for it notwithstanding? Can you who have such a heart, and have thus behaved yourself, come to God for any other than mere sovereign mercy?

II. If you should forever be cast off by God, it would be agreeable to your treatment of Jesus Christ. It would have been just with God if he had cast you off for ever, without ever making you the offer of a Savior.

But God hath not done that; he has provided a Savior for sinners, and offered him to you, even his own Son Jesus Christ, who is the only Savior of men. All that are not forever cast off are saved by him. God offers men salvation through him, and has promised us, that if we come to him, we shall not be cast off. But if you have treated, and still treat, this Savior after such a manner, that if you should be eternally cast off by God, it would be most agreeable to your behavior towards him; which appears by this, viz. "That you reject Christ, and will not have him for your Savior."

If God offers you a Savior from deserved punishment, and you will not receive him, then surely it is just that you should go without a Savior. Or is God obliged, because you do not like this Savior, to provide you another? He has given an infinitely honour able and glorious person, even his only begotten Son, to be a sacrifice for sin, and so provided salvation; and this Savior is offered to you: now if you refuse to accept him, is God therefore unjust if he does not save you? Is he obliged to save you in a way of your own choosing, because you do not like the way of his choosing? Or will you charge Christ with injustice because he does not become your Savior, when at the same time you will not have him when he offers himself to you, and beseeches you to accept of him as your Savior?

I am sensible that by this time many persons are ready to object against this. If all should speak what they now think, we should hear a murmuring all over the meeting-house, and one and another would say,

> I cannot see how this can be, that I am not willing that Christ should be my Savior, when I would give all the world that he was my Savior: how is it possible that I should not be willing to have Christ for my Savior when this is what I am seeking after, and praying for, and striving for, as for my life?

Here therefore I would endeavor to convince you, that you are under a gross mistake in this matter. And, first, I would endeavor to show the grounds of your mistake. And secondly, to demonstrate to you, that you have rejected, and do wilfully reject, Jesus Christ.

1. *That you may see the weak grounds of your mistake, consider,*

First, there is a great deal of difference between a willingness not to be damned, and a being willing to receive Christ for your Savior. You have the former; there is no doubt of that: nobody supposes that you love misery so as to choose an eternity of it; and so doubtless you are willing to be saved from eternal misery. But that is a very different thing from being willing to come to Christ: persons very commonly mistake the one for the other, but they are quite two things. You may love the deliverance, but hate the deliverer. You tell of a willingness; but consider what is the object of that willingness. It does not respect Christ; the way of salvation by him is not at all the object of it; but it is wholly terminated on your escape from misery. The inclination of your will goes no further than self, it never reaches Christ. You are willing not to be miserable; that is, you love yourself, and there your will and choice terminate. And it is but a vain pretense and delusion to say or think, that you are willing to accept of Christ.

Secondly, there is certainly a great deal of difference between a forced compliance and a free willingness. Force and freedom cannot consist together. Now that willingness, whereby you think you are willing to have Christ for a Savior, is merely a forced thing. Your heart does not go out after Christ of itself, but you are forced and driven to seek an interest in him. Christ has no share at all in your heart; there is no manner of closing of the heart with him. This forced compliance is not what Christ seeks of you; he seeks a free and willing acceptance. Psalm 110:3: "Thy people shall be willing in the day of thy power." He seeks not that you should receive him against your will, but with a free will. He seeks entertainment in your heart and choice. And if you refuse thus to receive Christ, how just is it that Christ should refuse to receive you? How reasonable are Christ's terms, who offers to save all those that willingly, or with a good will, accept of him for their Savior! Who can rationally expect that Christ should force himself upon any man to be his Savior? Or what can be looked for more reasonable, than that all who would be saved by Christ, should heartily and freely entertain him? And surely it would be very dishonorable for Christ to offer himself upon lower terms.

2. *But I would now proceed, secondly, to show that you are not willing to have Christ for a Savior.* To convince you of it, consider,

First, how it is possible that you should be willing to accept of Christ as a Savior from the desert of a punishment that you are not sensible you have deserved. If you are truly willing to accept of Christ as a Savior, it must be as a sacrifice to make atonement for your guilt. Christ came into the world on this errand, to offer himself as an atonement, to answer for our desert of punishment. But how can you be willing to have Christ for a Savior from a desert of Hell, if you be not sensible that you have a desert of Hell? If you have not really deserved everlasting burnings in Hell, then the very offer of an atonement for such a desert is an imposition upon you. If you have no such guilt upon you, then the very offer of a satisfaction for that guilt is an injury, because it implies in it a charge of guilt that you are free from. Now therefore it is impossible that a man who is not convinced of his guilt can be willing to accept of such an offer; because he cannot be willing to accept the charge which the offer implies. A man who is not convinced that he has deserved so dreadful a punishment, cannot willingly submit to be charged with it. If he thinks he is willing, it is but a mere forced, feigned business; because in his heart he looks upon himself greatly injured; and therefore he cannot freely accept of Christ, under that notion of a Savior from the desert of such a punishment; for such an acceptance is an implicit owning that he does deserve such a punishment.

I do not say, but that men may be willing to be saved from an undeserved punishment; they may rather not suffer it, than suffer it. But a man cannot be willing to accept one at God's hands, under the notion of a Savior from a punishment deserved from him which he thinks he has not deserved; it is impossible that anyone should freely allow a Savior under that notion. Such an one cannot like the way of salvation by Christ; for if he thinks he has not deserved Hell, then he will think that freedom from Hell is a debt; and therefore cannot willingly and heartily receive it as a free gift.

If a king should condemn a man to some tormenting death, which the condemned person thought himself not deserving of, but looked upon the sentence as unjust and cruel, and the king, when the time of execution drew nigh, should offer him his pardon, under the notion of a very great act of grace and clemency, the condemned person never could willingly and heartily allow it under that notion, because he judged himself unjustly condemned.

Now by this it is evident that you are not willing to accept of Christ as your Savior; because you never yet had such a sense of your own sinfulness, and such a conviction of your great guilt in God's sight, as to be indeed convinced that you lay justly condemned to the punishment of Hell. You never were convinced that you had forfeited all favor, and were in God's hands, and at his sovereign and arbitrary disposal, to be either destroyed or saved, just as he pleased. You never yet were convinced of the sovereignty of God. Hence are there so many objections arising against the justice of your punishment from original sin, and from God's decree, from mercy shown to others, and the like.

Secondly, that you are not sincerely willing to accept of Christ as your Savior, appears by this: that you never have been convinced that he is sufficient for the work of your salvation. You never had a sight or sense of any such excellency or worthiness in Christ, as should give such great value to his blood and his mediation with God, as that it was sufficient to be accepted for such exceeding guilty creatures, who have so provoked God, and exposed themselves to such amazing wrath. Saying it is so and allowing it be as others say, is a very different thing from being really convinced of it, and of being made sensible of it in your own heart. The sufficiency of Christ depends upon, or rather consists in, his excellency. It is because he is so excellent a person that his blood is of sufficient value to atone for sin, and it is hence that his obedience is so worthy in God's sight; it is also hence that his intercession is so prevalent; and therefore those that never had any spiritual sight or sense of Christ's excellency, cannot be sensible of his sufficiency.

And that sinners are not convinced that Christ is sufficient for the work he has undertaken, appears most manifestly when they are under great convictions of their sin, and danger of God's wrath. Though it may be before they thought they could allow Christ to be sufficient, (for it is easy to allow anyone to be sufficient for our defense at a time when we see no danger,) yet when they come to be sensible of their guilt and God's wrath, what discouraging thoughts do they entertain! How are they ready to draw towards despair, as if there were no hope or help for such wicked creatures as they! The reason is, they have no apprehension or sense of any other way that God's majesty can be vindicated, but only in their misery. To tell them of the blood of Christ signifies nothing, it does not relieve their sinking, despairing hearts. This makes it most evident that they are not convinced that Christ is sufficient to be their Mediator. And as long as they are unconvinced of this, it is impossible they should be willing to accept of him as their Mediator and Savior. A man in distressing fear will not willingly betake himself to a fort that he judges not sufficient to defend him from the enemy. A man will not willingly venture out into the ocean in a ship that he suspects is leaky, and will sink before he gets through his voyage.

3. *It is evident that you are not willing to have Christ for your Savior, because you have so mean an opinion of him, that you durst not trust his faithfulness.* One that undertakes to be the Savior of souls had need be faithful; for if he fails in such a trust, how great is the loss! But you are not convinced of Christ's faithfulness; as is evident, because at such times as when you are in a considerable measure sensible of your guilt and God's anger, you cannot be convinced that Christ is willing to accept of you, or that he stands ready to receive you, if you should come to him, though Christ so much invites you to come to him, and has so fully declared that he will not reject you, if you do come; as particularly. John 6:37: "Him that cometh to me, I will in no wise cast out." Now, there is no man can be heartily willing to trust his eternal welfare in the hands of an unfaithful person, or one whose faithfulness he suspects.

4. *You are not willing to be saved in that way by Christ, as is evident, because you are not willing that your own goodness should be set at nought.* In the way of salvation by Christ, men's own goodness is wholly set at nought; there is no account at all made of it. Now you cannot be willing to be saved in a way wherein your own goodness is set at nought, as is evident, since you make much of it yourself. You make much of your prayers and pains in religion, and are often thinking of them; how considerable do they appear to you, when you look back upon them! And some of you are thinking how much more you have done than others, and expecting some respect or regard that God should manifest to what you do. Now, if you make so much of what you do yourself, it is impossible that you should be freely willing that God should make nothing of it. As we may see in other things; if a man is proud of a great estate, or if he values himself much upon his honour able office, or his great abilities, it is impossible that he should like it, and heartily approve of it, that others should make light of these things and despise them.

Seeing therefore it is so evident, that you refuse to accept of Christ as your Savior, why is Christ to be blamed that he does not save you? Christ has offered himself to you, to be your Savior in time past, and he continues offering himself still, and you continue to reject him, and yet complain that he does not save you. So strangely unreasonable, and inconsistent with themselves, are gospel sinners!

But I expect there are many of you that still object. Such an objection as this, is probably now in the hearts of many here present.

Objection. If I am not willing to have Christ for my Savior, I cannot make myself willing.

But I would give an answer to this objection by laying down two things, that must be acknowledged to be exceeding evident.

1. *It is no excuse, that you cannot receive Christ of yourself, unless you would if you could.* This is so evident of itself, that it scarce needs any proof. Certainly if persons would not if they could, it is just the same thing as to the blame that lies upon them, whether they can or cannot. If you were willing, and then found that you could not, your being unable would alter the case, and might be some excuse; because then the defect would not be in your will, but only in your ability. But as long as you will not, it is no matter, whether you have ability or no ability.

If you are not willing to accept of Christ, it follows that you have no sincere willingness to be *willing*; because the will always necessarily approves of and rests in its own acts. To suppose the contrary, would be to suppose a contradiction; it would be to suppose that a man's will is contrary to itself, or that he wills contrary to what he himself wills. As you are not willing to come to Christ, and cannot make yourself willing, so you have no sincere desire to be willing; and therefore may most justly perish without a Savior. There is no excuse at all for you; for, say what you will about your inability, the seat of your blame lies in your perverse will, that is an enemy to the Savior. It is in vain for you to tell of your want of power, as long as your will is found defective. If a man should hate you, and smite you in the face, but should tell you at the same time, that he hated you so much, that he could not help choosing and willing so to do, would you take it the more patiently for that? Would not your indignation be rather stirred up the more?

2. If you would be willing if you could, that is no excuse, unless your unwilling-ness to be willing be sincere. That which is hypocritical, and does not come from the heart, but is merely forced, ought wholly to be set aside, as worthy of no consideration; because common sense teaches, that what is not hearty, but hypocritical is indeed nothing, being only a show of what is not; but that which is good for nothing, ought to go for nothing. But if you set aside all that is not free, and call nothing a willingness, but a free hearty will-ingness, then see how the case stands, and whether or no you have not lost all your excuse for standing out against the calls of the gospel. You say you would make yourself willing to accept if you could; but it is not from any good principle that you are willing for that. It is not from any free inclina-tion, or true respect to Christ, or any love to your duty, or any spirit of obe-dience. It is not from the influence of any real respect, or tendency in your heart, towards anything good, or from any other principle than such as is in the hearts of devils, and would make them have the same sort of willing-ness in the same circumstances. It is therefore evident, that there can be no goodness in that would be willing to come to Christ: and that which has no goodness, cannot be an excuse for any badness. If there be no good in it, then it signifies nothing, and weighs nothing, when put into the scales to counterbalance that which is bad.

Sinners therefore spend their time in foolish arguing and objecting, mak-ing much of that which is good for nothing, making those excuses that are not worth offering. It is in vain to keep making objection. You stand justly con-demned. The blame lies at your door: thrust it off from you as often as you will, it will return upon you. Sew fig-leaves as long as you will, your nakedness will appear. You continue wilfully and wickedly rejecting Jesus Christ, and will not have him for your Savior, and therefore it is sottish madness in you to charge Christ with injustice that he does not save you.

Here is the sin of unbelief! Thus the guilt of that great sin lies upon you! If you never had thus treated a Savior, you might most justly have been damned to all eternity: it would but be exactly agreeable to your treatment of God. But besides this, when God, notwithstanding, has of-fered you his own dear Son, to save you from this endless misery you had deserved, and not only so, but to make you happy eternally in the enjoy-ment of himself, you have refused him, and would not have him for your Savior, and still refuse to comply with the offers of the gospel; what can render any person more inexcusable? If you should now perish for ever, what can you have to say?

Hereby the justice of God in your destruction appears in two respects:

1. It is more abundantly manifest that it is just that you should be destroyed. Justice never appears so conspicuous as it does after refused and abused mercy. Justice in damnation appears abundantly the more clear and bright, after a wilful rejection of offered salvation. What can an offended prince do more than freely offer pardon to a condemned malefactor? And if he refuses to accept of it, will anyone say that his execution is unjust?

2. God's justice will appear in your greater destruction. Besides the guilt that you would have had if a Savior never had been offered, you bring that great additional guilt upon you, of most ungratefully refusing offered deliverance. What more base and vile treatment of God can there be, than for you, when justly condemned to eternal misery, and ready to be executed, and God graciously sends his own Son, who comes and knocks at your door with a pardon in his hand, and not only a pardon, but a deed of eternal glory; I say, what can be worse, than for you, out of dislike and enmity against God and his Son, to refuse to accept those benefits at his hands? How justly may the anger of God be greatly incensed and increased by it! When a sinner thus ungratefully rejects mercy, his last error is worse than the first; this is more heinous than all his former rebellion, and may justly bring down more fearful wrath upon him.

The heinousness of this sin of rejecting a Savior especially appears in two things:

1. The greatness of the benefits offered: which appears in the greatness of the deliverance, which is from inexpressible degrees of corruption and wickedness of heart and life, the least degree of which is infinitely evil; and from misery that is everlasting; and in the greatness and glory of the inheritance purchased and offered. Hebrews 2:3: "How shall we escape, if we neglect so great salvation."

2. The wonderfulness of the way in which these benefits are procured and offered. That God should lay help on his own Son, when our case was so deplorable that help could be had in no mere creature; and that he should undertake for us, and should come into the world, and take upon him our nature, and should not only appear in a low state of life, but should die such a death, and endure such torments and contempt for sinners while enemies—how wonderful is it! And what tongue or pen can set forth the greatness of the ingratitude, baseness, and perverseness there is in it, when a perishing sinner that is in the most extreme necessity of salvation, rejects it, after it is procured in such a way as this! That so glorious a person should be thus treated, and that when he comes on so gracious an errand! That he should stand so long offering himself and calling and inviting, as he has done to many of you, and all to no purpose, but all the while be set at nought! Surely you might justly be cast into Hell without one more offer of a Savior! Yea, and thrust down into the lowest Hell! Herein you have exceeded the very devils; for they never rejected the offers of such glorious mercy; no, nor of any mercy at all. This will be the distinguishing condemnation of gospel-sinners, John 3:18: "He that believeth not is condemned already, because he hath not believed in the name of the only begotten Son of God." That outward smoothness of your carriage towards Christ, that appearance of respect to him in your looks, your speeches, and gestures, do not argue but that you set him at nought in your heart. There may be much of these outward shows of respect, and yet you be like Judas, that betrayed the Son of man with a kiss; and like those mockers that bowed the knee before him, and at the same time spit in his face.

III. If God should forever cast you off and destroy you, it would be agreeable to your treatment of others.

It would be no other than what would be exactly answerable to your behavior towards your fellow-creatures, that have the same human nature, and are naturally in the same circumstances with you, and that you ought to love as yourself. And that appears especially in two things.

1. *You have many of you been opposite [opposed] in your spirit to the salvation of others.* There are several ways that natural men manifest a spirit of opposition against the salvation of souls. It sometimes appears by a fear that their companions, acquaintances, and equals, will obtain mercy, and so become unspeakably happier than they. It is sometimes manifested by an uneasiness at the news of what others have hopefully obtained. It appears when persons envy others for it, and dislike them the more, and disrelish their talk, and avoid their company, and cannot bear to hear their religious discourse, and especially to receive warnings and counsels from them. And it oftentimes appears by their backwardness to entertain charitable thoughts of them, and by their being brought with difficulty to believe that they have obtained mercy, and a forwardness to listen to anything that seems to contradict it. The devil hated to own Job's sincerity, Job 1:7, etc. and chapter 2, verses 3, 4, 5. There appears very often much of this spirit of the devil in

natural men. Sometimes they are ready to make a ridicule of others' pretended godliness; they speak of the ground of others' hopes, as the enemies of the Jews did of the wall that they built. Nehemiah 4:3. "Now Tobiah the Ammonite was by him, and he said, 'That which they build, if a fox go up, he shall even break down their stone wall.' " There are many that join with Sanballat and Tobiah, and are of the same spirit with them. There always was, and always will be, an enmity betwixt the seed of the serpent and the seed of the women. It appeared in Cain, who hated his brother, because he was more acceptable to God than himself; and it appears still in these times, and in this place. There are many that are like the elder brother, who could not bear that the prodigal, when he returned, should be received with such joy and good entertainment, and was put into a fret by it, both against his brother that had returned, and his father that had made him so welcome (Luke 15).

Thus have many of you been opposite to the salvation of others, who stand in as great necessity of it as you. You have been against their being delivered from everlasting misery, who can bear it no better than you; not because their salvation would do you any hurt, or their damnation help you, any otherwise than as it would gratify that vile spirit that is so much like the spirit of the devil, who, because he is miserable himself, is unwilling that others should be happy.

How just therefore is it that God should be opposite to your salvation! If you have so little love or mercy in you as to begrudge your neighbor's salvation, whom you have no cause to hate, but the law of God and nature requires you to love, why is God bound to exercise such infinite love and mercy to you, as to save you at the price of his own blood? You, whom he is no way bound to love, but who have deserved his hatred a thousand and a thousand times? You are not willing that others should be converted, who have behaved themselves injuriously towards you; and yet, will you count it hard if God does not bestow converting grace upon you that have deserved ten thousand times as ill of God, as ever any of your neighbors have of you? You are opposite to God's showing mercy to those that you think have been vicious persons, and are very unworthy of such mercy. Is others' unworthiness a just reason why God should not bestow mercy on them? And yet will God be hard, if, notwithstanding all your unworthiness, and the abominableness of your spirit and practice in his sight, he does not show you mercy? You would have God bestow liberally on you, and upbraid not; but yet when he shows mercy to others, you are ready to upbraid as soon as you hear of it; you immediately are thinking with yourself how ill they have behaved themselves; and it may be your mouths on this occasion are open, enumerating and aggravating the sins they have been guilty of. You would have God bury all your faults, and wholly blot out all your transgressions; but yet if he bestows mercy on others, it may be you will take that occasion to rake up all their old faults that you can think of. You do not much reflect on and condemn yourself for your baseness and unjust spirit towards others, in your opposition to their salvation; you do not quarrel with yourself, and condemn yourself for this; but yet you in your heart will quarrel with God, and fret at his dispensations, because you think he seems opposite to showing mercy to you. One would think that the consideration of these things should forever stop your mouth.

2. *Consider how you have promoted others' damnation.* Many of you, by the bad examples you have set, by corrupting the minds of others, by your sinful conversation, by leading them into or strengthening them in sin, and by the mischief you have done in human society other ways that might be mentioned, have been guilty of those things that have tended to others' damnation. You have heretofore appeared on the side of sin and Satan, and have strengthened their interest, and have been many ways accessary to others' sins, have hardened their hearts, and thereby have done what has tended to the ruin of their souls.

Without doubt there are those here present who have been in a great measure the means of others' damnation. One man may really be a means of others' damnation as well as salvation. Christ charges the scribes and Pharisees with this—Matthew 23:13: "Ye shut up the kingdom of heaven against men; for ye neither go in yourselves, neither suffer ye them that are entering, to go in." We have no reason to think that this congregation has none in it who are cursed from day to day by poor souls that are roaring out in Hell, whose damnation they have been the means of, or have greatly contributed to. There are many who contribute to their own children's damnation, by neglecting their education, by setting them bad examples, and bringing them up in sinful ways. They take some care of their bodies, but take little care of their poor souls; they provide for them bread to eat, but deny them the bread of life, that their famishing souls stand in need of. And are there no such parents here who have thus treated their children? If their children be not gone to Hell, no thanks to them; it is not because they have not done what has tended to their destruction. Seeing therefore you have had no more regard to others' salvation, and have promoted their damnation, how justly might God leave you to perish yourself!

IV. If God should eternally cast you off, it would but be agreeable to your own behavior towards yourself; and that in two respects:

1. In being so careless of your own salvation. You have refused to take care for your salvation, as God has counseled and commanded you from time to time; and why may not God neglect it, now you seek it of him? Is God obliged to be more careful of your happiness, than you are either of your own happiness or his glory? Is God bound to take that care for you, out of love to you, that you will not take for yourself, either from love to yourself, or regard to his authority? How long, and how greatly, have you neglected the welfare of your precious soul, refusing to take pains and deny yourself, or put yourself a little out of your way for your salvation, while God has been calling upon you! Neither your duty to God, nor love to your own soul, were enough to induce you to do little things for your own eternal welfare; and yet do you now expect that God should do great things, putting forth almighty power, and exercising infinite mercy for it? You was urged to take care for your salvation, and not to put it off. You were told that was the best time before you grew older, and that it might be, if you would put it off, God would not hear you afterwards; but yet you would not hearken; you would run the venture of it. Now how justly might God order it so, that it should be too late, leaving you to seek in vain! You was told, that you would repent of it if you delayed; but you would not hear: how justly therefore may God give you cause to repent of it, by refusing to show you mercy now! If God sees you going on in ways contrary to his commands and his glory, and requires you to forsake them, and tells you that they tend to the destruction of your own soul, and therefore counsels you to avoid them, and you refuse; how just would it be if God should be provoked by it, henceforward to be as careless of the good of your soul as you are yourself!

2. You have not only neglected your salvation, but you have wilfully taken direct courses to undo yourself. You have gone on in those ways and practices which have directly tended to your damnation, and have been perverse and obstinate it. You cannot plead ignorance; you had all the light set before you that you could desire. God told you that you was undoing yourself; but yet you would do it. He told you that the path you was going in led to destruction, and counseled you to avoid it; but you would not hearken. How justly therefore may God leave you to be undone! You have obstinately persisted to travel in the way that leads to Hell for a long time, contrary to God's continual counsels and commands, till it may be at length you are got almost to your journey's end, and are come near to Hell's gate, and so begin to be sensible of your danger and misery; and not account it unjust and hard if God will not deliver you! You have destroyed yourself, and destroyed yourself wilfully, contrary to God's repeated counsels, yea, and destroyed yourself in fighting against God. Now therefore, why do you blame any but yourself if you are destroyed? If you will undo yourself in opposing God, and while God opposes you by his calls and counsels, and, it may be too, by the convictions of his Spirit, what can you object against it, if God now leaves you to be undone? You would have your own way, and did not like that God should oppose you in it, and your way was to ruin your own soul; how just therefore is it, if, now at length, God ceases to oppose you, and falls in with you, and lets your soul be ruined; and as you would destroy yourself, so should put to his hand to destroy you too! The ways you went on in had a natural tendency to your misery: if you would drink poison in opposition to God, and in contempt of him and his advice, who can you blame but yourself if you are poisoned, and so perish? If you would run into the fire against all restraints both of God's mercy and authority, you must even blame yourself if you are burnt.

Thus I have proposed some things to your consideration, which, if you are not exceeding blind, senseless, and perverse, will stop your mouth, and convince you that you stand justly condemned before God; and that he would in no wise deal hardly with you, but altogether justly, in denying you any mercy, and in refusing to hear your prayers, though you pray never so earnestly, and never so often, and continue in it never so long. God may utterly disregard your tears and moans, your heavy heart, your earnest desires, and great endeavors; and he may cast you into eternal destruction, without any regard to your welfare, denying you converting grace, and giving you over to Satan, and at last cast you into the lake that burns with fire and brimstone, to be there to eternity, having no rest day or night, forever glorifying his justice upon you in the presence of the holy angels, and in the presence of the Lamb.

Objection. But here many may still object, (for I am sensible it is a hard thing to stop sinners' mouths,) "God shows mercy to others that have done these things as well as I, yea, that have done a great deal worse than I."

Answer. 1. That does not prove that God is any way bound to show mercy to you, or them either. If God bestows it on others, he does not so because he is bound to bestow it: he might if he had pleased, with glorious justice, have denied it them. If God bestows it on some, that does not prove that he is bound to bestow it on any; and if he is bound to bestow it on none, then he is not bound to bestow it on you. God is in debt to none; and if he gives to some that he is not in debt to, because it is his pleasure, that does not bring him into debt to others. It alters not the case as to you, whether others have it, or have it not: you do not deserve damnation the less, than if mercy never had been bestowed on any at all. Matthew 20:15: "Is thine eye evil, because mine is good?"

2. *If this objection be good, then the exercise of God's mercy is not in his own right, and his grace is not his own to give.* That which God may not dispose of as he pleases, is not his own; for that which is one's own, is at his own disposal: but if it be not God's own, then he is not capable of making a gift or present of it to anyone; it is impossible to give what is a debt. What is it that you would make of God? Must the great God be tied up, that he must not use his own pleasure in bestowing his own gifts, but if he bestows them on one, must be looked upon obliged to bestow them on another? Is not God worthy to have the same right, with respect to the gifts of his grace, that a man has to his money or goods? Is it because God is not so great, and should be more in subjection than man, that this cannot be allowed him? If any of you see cause to show kindness to a neighbor, do all the rest of your neighbors come to you, and tell you, that you owe them so much as you have given to such a man? But this is the way that you deal with God, as though God were not worthy to have as absolute a property in his goods, as you have in yours.

At this rate God cannot make a present of anything; he has nothing of his own to bestow: if he has a mind to show peculiar favor to some, or to lay some particular persons under peculiar obligations to him, he cannot do it; because he has no special gift at his own disposal. If this be the case, why do you pray to God to bestow saving grace upon you? If God does not do fairly to deny it you, because he bestows it on others, then it is not worth your while to pray for it, but you may go and tell him that he has bestowed it on others as bad or worse than you, and so demand it of him as a debt. And at this rate persons never need to thank God for salvation, when it is bestowed; for what occasion is there to thank God for that which was not at his own disposal, and that he could not fairly have denied? The thing at bottom is, that men have low thoughts of God, and high thoughts of themselves; and therefore it is that they look upon God as having so little right, and they so much. Matthew 20:15. "Is it not lawful for me to do what I will with mine own?"

3. God may justly show greater respect to others than to you, for you have shown greater respect to others than to God. You have rather chosen to offend God than men. God only shows a greater respect to others, who are by nature your equals, than to you; but you have shown a greater respect to those that are infinitely inferior to God than to him. You have shown a greater regard to wicked men than to God; you have honored them more, loved them better, and adhered to them rather than to him. Yea, you have honored the devil, in many respects, more than God: you have chosen his will and his interest, rather than God's will and his glory: you have chosen a little worldly pelf [cash], rather than God: you have set more by a vile lust than by him: you have chosen these things, and rejected God. You have set your heart on these things, and cast God behind your back: and where is the injustice if God is pleased to show greater respect to others than to you, or if he chooses others and rejects you? You have shown greater respect to vile and worthless things, and no respect to God's glory; and why may not God set his love on others, and have no respect to your happiness? You have shown great respect to others, and not to God, whom you are laid under infinite obligations to respect above all; and why may not God show respect to others, and not to you, who never have laid him under the least obligation?

And will you not be ashamed, notwithstanding all these things, still to open your mouth, to object and cavil about the decrees of God, and other things that you cannot fully understand. Let the decrees of God be what they will, that alters not the case as to your liberty, any more than if God had only foreknown. And why is God to blame for decreeing things? Especially since he decrees nothing but good. How unbecoming an infinitely wise Being would it have been to have made a world, and let things run at random, without disposing events, or fore-ordering how they should come to pass? And what is that to you, how God has fore-ordered things, as long as your constant experience teaches you, that it does not hinder your doing what you choose to do. This you know, and your daily practice and behavior amongst men declares that you are fully sensible of it with respect to yourself and others. Still to object, because there are some things in God's dispensations above your understanding, is exceedingly unreasonable. Your own conscience charges you with great guilt, and with those things that have been mentioned, let the secret things of God be what they will. Your conscience charges you with those vile dispositions, and that base behavior towards God, that you would at any time most highly resent in your neighbor towards you, and that not a whit the less for any concern those secret counsels and mysterious dispensations of God may have in the matter. It is in vain for you to exalt yourself against an infinitely great, and holy, and just God. If you continue in it, it will be to your eternal shame and confusion, when hereafter you shall see at whose door all the blame of your misery lies.

I will finish what I have to say to natural men in the application of this doctrine, with a caution not to improve the doctrine to discouragement. For though it would be righteous in God forever to cast you off, and destroy you, yet it would also be just in God to save you, in and through Christ, who has made complete satisfaction for all sin. Romans 3:25, 26:

> Whom God hath set forth to be a propitiation, through faith in his blood, to declare his righteousness for the remission of sins that are past, through the forbearance of God; to declare, I say, at this time his righteousness, that he might be just, and the justifier of him which believeth in Jesus.

Yea, God may, through this Mediator, not only justly, but honorably, show you mercy. The blood of Christ is so precious, that it is fully sufficient to pay the debt you have contracted, and perfectly to vindicate the Divine Majesty from all the dishonor cast upon it, by these many great sins of yours that have been mentioned. It was as great, and indeed a much greater thing, for Christ to die, than it would have been for you and all mankind to have burnt in Hell to all eternity. Of such dignity and excellency is Christ in the eyes of God, that, seeing he has suffered so much for poor sinners, God is willing to be at peace with them, however vile and unworthy they have been, and on how many accounts soever the punishment would be just. So that you need not be at all discouraged from seeking mercy, for there is enough in Christ.

Indeed it would not become the glory of God's majesty to show mercy to you, so sinful and vile a creature, for anything that you have done; for such worthless and despicable things as your prayers, and other religious performances. It would be very dishonorable and unworthy of God so to do, and it is in vain to expect it. He will show mercy only on Christ's account; and that, according to his sovereign pleasure, on whom he pleases, when he pleases, and in what manner he pleases. You cannot bring him under obligation by your works; do what you will, he will not look on himself obliged. But if it be his pleasure, he can honorably show mercy through Christ to any sinner of you all, not one in this congregation excepted. Therefore here is encouragement for you still to seek and wait, notwithstanding all your wickedness; agreeable to Samuel's speech to the children of Israel, when they were terrified with the thunder and rain that God sent, and when guilt stared them in the face. 1 Samuel 12:20: "Fear not; ye have done all this wickedness; yet turn not aside from following the Lord, but serve the Lord with all your heart."

I would conclude this discourse by putting the godly in mind of the freeness and wonderfulness of the grace of God towards them. For such were the same of you. The case was just so with you as you have heard; you had such a wicked heart, you lived such a wicked life, and it would have been most just with God forever to have cast you off: but he has had mercy upon you; he hath made his glorious grace appear in your everlasting salvation. You had no love to God; but yet he has exercised unspeakable love to you. You have contemned [viewed with contempt] God, and set light by him: but so great a value has God's grace set on you and your happiness, that you have been redeemed at the price of the blood of his own Son. You chose to be with Satan in his service; but yet God hath made you a joint heir with Christ of his glory. You was ungrateful for past mercies; yet God not only continued those mercies, but bestowed unspeakably greater mercies upon you. You refused to hear when God called; yet God heard you when you called. You abused the infiniteness of God's mercy to encourage yourself in sin against him; yet God has manifested the infiniteness of that mercy, in the exercises of it towards you. You have rejected Christ, and set him at nought; and yet he is become your Savior. You have neglected your own salvation; but God has not neglected it. You have destroyed yourself; but yet in God has been your help. God has magnified his free grace towards you, and not to others; because he has chosen you, and it hath pleased him to set his love upon you.

O! what cause is here for praise! What obligations you are under to bless the Lord who hath dealt bountifully with you, and magnify his holy name! What cause for you to praise God in humility, to walk humbly before him. Ezekiel 16:63:

> That thou mayest remember and be confounded, and never open thy mouth any more, because of thy shame, when I am pacified toward thee for all that thou hast done, saith the Lord God!

You shall never open your mouth in boasting, or self-justification; but lie the lower before God for his mercy to you. You have reason, the more abundantly, to open your mouth in God's praises, that they may be continually in your mouth, both here and to all eternity, for his rich, unspeakable, and sovereign mercy to you, whereby he, and he alone, hath made you to differ from others.

Pressing into the Kingdom of God

February 1735. "This . . . sermon has uncommon ardor, unction, and solemnity, and was one of the most useful which he delivered." (*Memoirs of Jonathan Edwards*)

"The law and the prophets were until John; since that time the kingdom of God is preached, and every man presseth into it."—Luke 16:16

In these words two things may be observed.

First, *wherein the work and office of John the Baptist consisted, viz. in preaching the kingdom of God, to prepare the way for its introduction to succeed the law and the prophets.* By "the law and the prophets," in the text, seems to be intended the ancient dispensation under the Old Testament, which was received from Moses and the prophets. These are said to be until John; not that the revelations given by them are out of use since that time, but that the state of the church, founded and regulated under God by them, the dispensation of which they were the ministers, and wherein the church depended mainly on light received from them, fully continued till John. He first began to introduce the New Testament dispensation, or gospel-state of the church; which, with its glorious, spiritual, and eternal privileges and blessings, is often called the kingdom of heaven, or kingdom of God. John the Baptist preached that the kingdom of God was at hand. "Repent" says he, "for the kingdom of heaven is at hand." "Since that time," says Christ, "the kingdom of God is preached." John the Baptist first began to preach it; and then, after him, Christ and his disciples preached the same.

Thus Christ preached, Matthew 4:17: "From that time Jesus began to preach, and to say, 'Repent, for the kingdom of heaven is at hand.' " So the disciples were directed to preach, Matthew 10:7: "And, as ye go, preach, saying, 'The kingdom of heaven is at hand.' " It was not John the Baptist, but Christ, that fully brought in, and actually established, this kingdom of God; but he [John], as Christ's forerunner to prepare his way before him, did the first thing that was done towards introducing it. The old dispensation was abolished, and the new brought in by degrees; as the night gradually ceases, and gives place to the increasing day which succeeds in its room.

First the day-star arises; next follows the light of the sun itself, but dimly reflected, in the dawning of the day; but this light increases, and shines more and more, and the stars that served for light during the foregoing night, gradually go out, and their light ceases, as being now needless, till at length the sun rises, and enlightens the world by his own direct light, which increases as he ascends higher above the horizon, till the day-star itself gradually disappears. [This is] agreeable to what John says of himself, John 3:30: "He must increase, but I must decrease." John was the forerunner of Christ, and harbinger of the gospel-day; much as the morning-star is the forerunner of the sun. He had the most honorable office of any of the prophets; the other prophets foretold Christ to come: he revealed him as already come, and had the honor to be that servant who should come immediately before him, and actually introduce him, and even to be the instrument concerned in his solemn inauguration, as he was in baptizing him. He was the greatest of the prophets that came before Christ, as the morning-star is the brightest of all the stars, Matthew 11:11. He came to prepare men's hearts to receive that kingdom of God which Christ was about more fully to reveal and erect. Luke 1:17: "To make ready a people prepared for the Lord."

Secondly, we may observe wherein his success appeared, viz. in that since he began his ministry, every man pressed into that kingdom of God which he preached. The greatness of his success appeared in two things:

- *In the generalness of it, with regard to the subject, or the persons in whom the success appeared; every man.* Here is a term of universality; but it is not to be taken as universal with regard to individuals, but kinds; as such universal terms are often used in Scripture. When John preached, there was an extraordinary pouring out of the Spirit of God that attended his preaching. An uncommon awakening, and concern for salvation, appeared on the minds of all sorts of persons; and even in the most unlikely persons, and those from whom such a thing might least be expected; as the Pharisees, who were exceeding proud, and self-sufficient, and conceited of their own wisdom and righteousness, and looked on themselves fit to be teachers of others, and used to scorn to be taught; and the Sadducees, who were a kind of infidels, that denied any resurrection, angel, spirit, or any future state. So that John himself seems to be surprised to see them come to him, under such concern for their salvation; as in Matthew 3:7.

> But when he saw many of the Pharisees come to his baptism, he said to them, "O generation of vipers, who hath warned you to flee from the wrath to come?"

And besides these, the publicans, who were some of the most infamous sort of men, came to him, inquiring what they should do to be saved. And the soldiers, who were doubtless a very profane, loose, and profligate sort of persons, made the same inquiry, Luke 3:12 and 14.

> Then came also publicans to be baptized, and said unto him, "Master, what shall we do?" And the soldiers likewise demanded of him, saying, "And what shall we do?"

- *His success appeared in the manner in which his hearers sought the kingdom of God; they pressed into it.* It is elsewhere set forth by their being violent for the kingdom of heaven, and taking it by force. Matthew 11:12. "From the days of John the Baptist until now, the kingdom of heaven suffers violence, and the violent take it by force."

Doctrine

The doctrine that I observe from the words is this, "It concerns every one that would obtain the kingdom of God, to be pressing into it." In discoursing of this subject, I would,

I. Show what is that way of seeking salvation that seems to be pointed forth in the expression of pressing into the kingdom of God.

II. Give the reasons why it concerns every one that would obtain the kingdom of God, to seek it in this way.

III. Then make application.

I. I would show what manner of seeking salvation seems to be denoted by "pressing into the kingdom of God."

1. *This expression denotes strength of desire.* Men in general who live under the light of the gospel, and are not atheists, desire the kingdom of God; that is, they desire to go to heaven rather than to Hell. Most of them indeed are not much concerned about it; but on the contrary, live a secure and careless life. And some who are many degrees above these, being under some degrees of the awakenings of God's Spirit, yet are not pressing into the kingdom of God. But they that may be said to be truly so, have strong desires to get out of a natural condition, and to get an interest in Christ. They have such a conviction of the misery of their present state, and of the extreme necessity of obtaining a better, that their minds are, as it were, possessed with and wrapped up in concern about it.

To obtain salvation is desired by them above all things in the world. This concern is so great that it very much shuts out other concerns. They used before to have the stream of their desires after other things, or, it may be, had their concern divided between this and them; but when they come to answer the expression of the text, of pressing into the kingdom of God, this concern prevails above all others; it lays other things low, and does in a manner engross the care of the mind. This seeking eternal life should not only be one concern that our souls are taken up about with other things; but salvation should be sought as the one thing needful, Luke 10:42. And as the one thing that is desired, Psalm 27:4.

2. *Pressing into the kingdom of heaven denotes earnestness and firmness of resolution.* There should be strength of resolution, accompanying strength of desire, as it was in the psalmist, in the place just now referred to: "one thing have I desired, and that will I seek after." In order to a thorough engagedness of the mind in this affair, both these must meet together. Besides desires after salvation, there should be an earnest resolution in persons to pursue this good as much as lies in their power; to do all that in the use of their utmost strength they are able to do, in an attendance on every duty, and resisting and militating against all manner of sin, and to continue in such a pursuit.

There are two things needful in a person, in order to these strong resolutions; there must be a sense of the great importance and necessity of the mercy sought, and there must also be a sense of opportunity to obtain it, or the encouragement there is to seek it. The strength of resolution depends on the sense which God gives to the heart of these things. Persons without such a sense, may seem to themselves to take up resolutions; they may, as it were, force a promise to themselves, and say within themselves, "I will seek as long as I live, I will not give up till I obtain," when they do but deceive themselves. Their hearts are not in it; neither do they indeed take up any such resolution as they seem to themselves to do. It is the resolution of the mouth more than of the heart; their hearts are not strongly bent to fulfill what their mouth says. The firmness of the resolution lies in the fullness of the disposition of the heart to do what is resolved to be done. Those who are pressing into the kingdom of God, have a disposition of heart to do everything that is required, and that lies in their power to do, and to continue in it. They have not only earnestness, but steadiness of resolution: they do not seek with a wavering unsteady heart, by turns or fits, being off and on; but it is the constant bent of the soul, if possible, to obtain the kingdom of God.

3. *By pressing into the kingdom of God is signified greatness of endeavor.* It is expressed in Ecclesiastes 10:10, by doing what our hand finds to do with our might. And this is the natural and necessary consequence of the two aforementioned things. Where there is strength of desire, and firmness of resolution, there will be answerable endeavors. Persons thus engaged in their hearts will "strive to enter in at the strait gate," and will be violent for heaven; their practice will be agreeable to the counsel of the wise man, in Proverbs 2 at the beginning,

> My son, if thou wilt receive my words, and hide my commandments with thee; so that thou incline thine ear unto wisdom, and apply thine heart to understanding; yea, if thou criest after knowledge, and liftest up thy voice for understanding; if thou seekest her as silver, and searchest for her as for hid treasures; then shalt thou understand the fear of the Lord, and find the knowledge of God.

Here the earnestness of desire and strength of resolution is signified by inclining the ear to wisdom, and applying the heart to understanding; and the greatness of endeavor is denoted by crying after knowledge, and lifting up the voice for understanding; seeking her as silver, and searching for her as for hid treasures: such desires and resolutions, and such endeavors go together.

4. *Pressing into the kingdom of God denotes an engagedness and earnestness, that is directly about that business of getting into the kingdom of God.* Persons may be in very great exercise and distress of mind, and that about the condition of their souls; their thoughts and cares may be greatly engaged and taken up about things of a spiritual nature, and yet not be pressing into the

kingdom of God, nor towards it. The exercise of their minds is not directly about the work of seeking salvation, in a diligent attendance on the means that God hath appointed in order to it, but something else that is beside their business; it may be God's decrees and secret purposes, prying into them, searching for signs whereby they may determine, or at least conjecture, what they are before God makes them known by their accomplishment. They distress their minds with fears that they be not elected, or that they have committed the unpardonable sin, or that their day is past, and that God has given them up to judicial and final hardness, and never intends to show them mercy; and therefore, that it is in vain for them to seek salvation. Or they entangle themselves about the doctrine of original sin, and other mysterious doctrines of religion that are above their comprehension.

Many persons that seem to be in great distress about a future eternal state, get much into a way of perplexing themselves with such things as these. When it is so, let them be never so much concerned and engaged in their minds—they cannot be said to be pressing towards the kingdom of God: because their exercise is not in their work, but rather that which tends to hinder them in their work. If they are violent, they are only working violently to entangle themselves, and lay blocks in their own way; their pressure is not forwards. Instead of getting along, they do but lose their time, and worse than merely lose it; instead of fighting with the giants that stand in the way to keep them out of Canaan, they spend away their time and strength in conflicting with shadows that appear by the wayside.

Hence we are not to judge of the hopefulness of the way that persons are in, or of the probability of their success in seeking salvation, only by the greatness of the concern and distress that they are in; for many persons have needless distresses that they had much better be without. It is thus very often with persons overrun with the distemper of melancholy: whence the adversary of souls is wont to take great advantage. But then are persons in the most likely way to obtain the kingdom of heaven, when the intent of their minds, and the engagedness of their spirits, be about their proper work and business, and all the bent of their souls is to attend on God's means, and to do what he commands and directs them to. The apostle tells us, 1 Corrinthians 9:26, "that he did not fight as those that beat the air." Our time is short enough; we had not need to spend it in that which is nothing to the purpose. There are real difficulties and enemies enough for persons to encounter, to employ all their strength; they had not need to waste it in fighting with phantoms.

5. *By pressing into the kingdom of God is denoted a breaking through opposition and difficulties.* There is in the expression a plain intimation of difficulty. If there were no opposition, but the way was all clear and open, there would be no need of pressing to get along. They therefore that are pressing into the kingdom of God, go on with such engagedness, that they break through the difficulties that are in the way. They are so set for salvation, that those things by which others are discouraged, and stopped, and turned back, do not stop them, but they press through them. Persons ought to be so resolved for heaven, that if by any means they *can* obtain, they *will* obtain. Whether those means be difficult or easy, cross or agreeable, if they are requisite means of salvation, they should be complied with. When anything is presented to be done, the question should not be, "Is it easy or hard?" "Is it agreeable to my carnal inclinations or interest, or against them?" but "Is it a required means of my obtaining an interest in Jesus Christ, and eternal salvation?" Thus the apostle, Philippians 3:11. "If by any means I might attain unto the resurrection of the dead." He tells us there in the context what difficulties he broke through, that he suffered the loss of all things, and was willingly made conformable even to Christ's death, though that was attended with such extreme torment and ignominy.

He that is pressing into the kingdom of God, commonly finds many things in the way that are against the grain; but he is not stopped by the cross that lies before him, but takes it up, and carries it. Suppose there be something incumbent on him to do, that is cross to his natural temper, and irksome to him on that account; suppose something that he cannot do without suffering in his estate, or that he apprehends will look odd and strange in the eyes of others, and expose him to ridicule and reproach, or anything that will offend a neighbor, and get his ill-will, or something that will be very cross to his own carnal appetite—he will press through such difficulties. Everything that is found to be a weight that hinders him in running this race he casts from him, though it be a weight of gold or pearls; yea, if it be a right hand or foot that offends him, he will cut them off, and will not stick at plucking out a right eye with his own hands. These things are insuperable difficulties to those who are not thoroughly engaged in seeking their salvation; they are stumbling-blocks that they never get over. But it is not so with him that presses into the kingdom of God. Those things (before he was thoroughly roused from his security) about which he was wont to have long parleyings and disputings with his own conscience—employing carnal reason to invent arguments and pleas of excuse—he now sticks at no longer; he has done with this endless disputing and reasoning, and presses violently through all difficulties.

Let what will be in the way, heaven is what he must and will obtain, not if he can without difficulty, but if it be *possible*. He meets with temptation: the devil is often whispering in his ear, setting allurements before him, magnifying the difficulties of the work he is engaged in, telling him that they are insuperable, and that he can never conquer them, and trying all ways in the world to discourage him; but still he presses forward. God has given and maintains such an earnest spirit for heaven, that the devil cannot stop him in his course; he is not at leisure to lend an ear to what he has to say.

I come now,

II. To show why the kingdom of heaven should be sought in this manner.

It should be thus sought:

1. *On account of the extreme necessity we are in of getting into the kingdom of heaven.* We are in a perishing necessity of it; without it we are utterly and eternally lost. Out of the kingdom of God is no safety; there is no other hiding-place; this is the only city of refuge, in which we can be secure from the avenger that pursues all the ungodly. The vengeance of God will pursue, overtake, and eternally destroy, them that are not in this kingdom. All that are without this enclosure will be swallowed up in an overflowing fiery deluge of wrath. They may stand at the door and knock, and cry, "Lord, Lord, open to us," in vain; they will be thrust back; and God will have no mercy on them; they shall be eternally left of him. His fearful vengeance will seize them; the devils will lay hold of them; and all evil will come upon them; and there will be none to pity or help; their case will be utterly desperate, and infinitely doleful. It will be a gone case with them; all offers of mercy and expressions of divine goodness will be finally withdrawn, and all hope will be lost. God will have no kind of regard to their well-being; will take no care of them to save them from any enemy, or any evil; but himself will be their dreadful enemy, and will execute wrath with fury, and will take vengeance in an inexpressibly dreadful manner. Such as shall be in this case will be lost and undone indeed! They will be sunk down into perdition, infinitely below all that we can think. For who knows the power of God's anger? And who knows the misery of that poor worm, on whom that anger is executed without mercy?

2. *On account of the shortness and uncertainty of the opportunity for getting into this kingdom.* When a few days are past, all our opportunity for it will be gone. Our day is limited. God has set our bounds, and we know not where. While persons are out of this kingdom, they are in danger every hour of being overtaken with wrath. We know not how soon we shall get past that line, beyond which there is no work, device, knowledge, nor wisdom; and therefore we should do what we have to do with our might, Ecclesiastes 9:10.

3. *On account of the difficulty of getting into the kingdom of God.* There are innumerable difficulties in the way; such as few conquer: most of them that try have not resolution, courage, earnestness, and constancy enough; but they fail, give up, and perish. The difficulties are too many and too great for them that do not violently press forward. They never get along, but stick by the way; are turned aside, or turned back, and ruined. Matthew 7:14: "Strait is the gate, and narrow is the way, which leadeth unto life, and few there be that find it." Luke 13:24: "Strive to enter in at the strait gate; for many, I say unto you, will seek to enter in, and shall not be able."

4. *The possibility of obtaining.* Though it be attended with so much difficulty, yet it is not a thing impossible. Acts 8:22: "If perhaps the thought of thine heart may be forgiven thee." I1 Timothy 2:25: "If peradventure God will give them repentance to the acknowledging of the truth." However sinful a person is, and whatever his circumstances are, there is, notwithstanding, a possibility of his salvation. He himself is capable of it, and God is able to accomplish it, and has mercy sufficient for it; and there is sufficient provision made through Christ, that God may do it consistent with the honor of his majesty, justice, and truth. So that there is no want either of sufficiency in God, or capacity in the sinner, in order to this. The greatest and vilest most blind, dead, hard-hearted sinner living, is a subject capable of saving light and grace. Seeing therefore there is such a necessity of obtaining the kingdom of God, and so short a time, and such difficulty, and yet such a possibility, it may well induce us to press into it. (Jonah 3:8, 9.)

5. *It is meet that the kingdom of heaven should be thus sought, because of the great excellency of it.* We are willing to seek earthly things, of trifling value, with great diligence, and through much difficulty; it therefore certainly becomes us to seek that with great earnestness which is of infinitely greater worth and excellence. And how well may God expect and require it of us, that we should seek it in such a manner, in order to our obtaining it!

6. *Such a manner of seeking is needful to prepare persons for the kingdom of God.* Such earnestness and thoroughness of endeavors, is the ordinary

means that God makes use of to bring persons to an acquaintance with themselves, to a sight of their own hearts, to a sense of their own helplessness, and to a despair in their own strength and righteousness. And such engagedness and constancy in seeking the kingdom of heaven, prepare the soul to receive it the more joyfully and thankfully, and the more highly to prize and value it when obtained. So that it is in mercy to us, as well as for the glory of his own name, that God has appointed such earnest seeking, to be the way in which he will bestow the kingdom of heaven.

Application

The use I would make of this doctrine, is of exhortation to all Christless persons to press into the kingdom of God. Some of you are inquiring what you shall do? You seem to desire to know what is the way wherein salvation is to be sought, and how you may be likely to obtain it. You have now heard the way that the holy word of God directs to. Some are seeking, but it cannot be said of them that they are pressing into the kingdom of heaven. There are many that in time past have sought salvation, but not in this manner, and so they never obtained, but are now gone to Hell. Some of them sought it year after year, but failed of it, and perished at last. They were overtaken with divine wrath, and are now suffering the fearful misery of damnation, and have no rest day nor night, having no more opportunity to seek, but must suffer and be miserable throughout the never-ending ages of eternity. Be exhorted, therefore, not to seek salvation as they did, but let the kingdom of heaven suffer violence from you.

Here I would first answer an objection or two, and then proceed to give some directions how to press into the kingdom of God.

Objection 1. Some may be ready to say,

> We cannot do this of ourselves; that strength of desire, and firmness of resolution, that have been spoken of, are out of our reach. If I endeavor to resolve and to seek with engagedness of spirit, I find I fail; my thoughts are presently off from the business, and I feel myself dull, and my engagedness relaxed, in spite of all I can do.

Answer 1. Though earnestness of mind be not immediately in your power, yet the consideration of what has been now said of the need of it, may be a means of stirring you up to it. It is true, persons never will be thoroughly engaged in this business, unless it be by God's influence; but God influences persons by means. Persons are not stirred up to a thorough earnestness without some considerations that move them to it. And if persons can but be made sensible of the necessity of salvation, and also duly consider the exceeding difficulty of it, and the greatness of the opposition, and how short and uncertain the time is, but yet are sensible that they have an opportunity, and that there is a possibility of their obtaining, they will need no more in order to their being thoroughly engaged and resolved in this matter. If we see persons slack and unresolved, and unsteady, it is because they do not enough consider these things.

Answer 2. Though strong desires and resolutions of mind be not in your power, yet painfulness of endeavors is in your power. It is in your power to take pains in the use of means, yea very great pains. You can be very painful and diligent in watching your own heart, and striving against sin. Though there is all manner of corruption in the heart continually ready to work, yet you can very laboriously watch and strive against these corruptions; and it is in your power, with great diligence to attend the matter of your duty towards God and towards your neighbor. It is in your power to attend all ordinances, and all public and private duties of religion, and to do it with your might.

It would be a contradiction to suppose that a man cannot do these things with all the might he has, though he cannot do them with more might than he has. The dullness and deadness of the heart, and slothfulness of disposition, do not hinder men being able to take pains, though it hinders their being willing. That is one thing wherein your laboriousness may appear, even striving against your own dullness. That men have a dead and sluggish heart, does not argue that they be not able to take pains; it is so far from that, that it gives occasion for pains. It is one of the difficulties in the way of duty, that persons have to strive with, and that gives occasion for struggling and labor.

If there were no difficulties attended seeking salvation, there would be no occasion for striving; a man would have nothing to strive about. There is indeed a great deal of difficulty attending all duties required of those that would obtain heaven. It is an exceeding difficult thing for them to keep their thoughts; it is a difficult thing seriously, or to any good purpose, to consider matters of greatest importance; it is a difficult thing to hear, or read, or pray attentively. But it does not argue that a man cannot strive in these things because they are difficult; nay, he could not strive therein if there were not difficulty in them. For what is there excepting difficulties that any can have to strive or struggle with in any affair or business? Earnestness of mind, and diligence of endeavor, tend to promote each other.

He that has a heart earnestly engaged, will take pains; and he that is diligent and painful in all duty, probably will not be so long before he finds the sensibleness of his heart and earnestness of his spirit greatly increased.

Objection 2. Some may object, that if they are earnest, and take a great deal of pains, they shall be in danger of trusting to what they do; they are afraid of doing their duty for fear of making a righteousness of it.

Answer. There is ordinarily no kind of seekers that trust so much to what they do, as slack and dull seekers. Though all seeking salvation, that have never been the subjects of a thorough humiliation, do trust in their own righteousness; yet some do it much more fully than others. Some though they trust in their own righteousness, yet are not quiet in it. And those who are most disturbed in their self-confidence, (and therefore in the likeliest way to be wholly brought off from it,) are not such as go on in a remiss way of seeking, but such as are most earnest and thoroughly engaged; partly because in such a way conscience is kept more sensible. A more awakened conscience will not rest so quietly in moral and religious duties, as one that is less awakened. A dull seeker's conscience will be in a great measure satisfied and quieted with his own works and performances; but one that is thoroughly awakened cannot be stilled or pacified with such things as these. In this way persons gain much more knowledge of themselves, and acquaintance with their own hearts, than in a negligent, slight way of seeking; for they have a great deal more experience of themselves. It is experience of ourselves, and finding what we are, that God commonly makes use of as the means of bringing us off from all dependence on ourselves. But men never get acquaintance with themselves so fast, as in the most earnest way of seeking. They that are in this way have more to engage them to think of their sins, and strictly to observe themselves, and have much more to do with their own hearts, than others. Such a one has much more experience of his own weakness, than another that does not put forth and try his strength; and will therefore sooner see himself dead in sin. Such a one, though he hath a disposition continually to be flying to his own righteousness, yet finds rest in nothing; he wanders about from one thing to another, seeking something to ease his disquieted conscience; he is driven from one refuge to another, goes from mountain to hill, seeking rest and finding none; and therefore will the sooner prove that there is no rest to be found, nor trust to be put, in any creature whatsoever.

It is therefore quite a wrong notion that some entertain, that the more they do, the more they shall depend on it. Whereas the reverse is true; the more they do, or the more thorough they are in seeking, the less will they be likely to rest in their doings, and the sooner will they see the vanity of all that they do. So that persons will exceedingly miss it, if ever they neglect to do any duty either to God or man, whether it be any duty of religion, justice, or charity, under a notion of its exposing them to trust in their own righteousness. It is very true, that it is a common thing for persons, when they earnestly seek salvation, to trust in the pains that they take: but yet commonly those that go on in a more slight way, trust a great deal more securely to their dull services, than he that is pressing into the kingdom of God does to his earnestness. Men's slackness in religion, and their trust in their own righteousness, strengthen and establish one another. Their trust in what they have done, and what they now do, settles them in a slothful rest and ease, and hinders their being sensible of their need of rousing up themselves and pressing forward. And on the other hand, their negligence tends so to benumb them in such ignorance of themselves, that the most miserable refuges are stupidly rested in as sufficient. Therefore we see, that when persons have been going on for a long time in such a way, and God afterwards comes more thoroughly to awaken them, and to stir them up to be in good earnest, he shakes all their old foundations, and rouses them out of their old resting places; so that they cannot quiet themselves with those things that formerly kept them secure.

I. I would now proceed to give some directions how you should press into the kingdom of God.

1. *Be directed to sacrifice every thing to your soul's eternal interest.* Let seeking this be so much your bent, and what you are so resolved in, that you will make every thing give place to it. Let nothing stand before your resolution of seeking the kingdom of God. Whatever it be that you used to look upon as a convenience, or comfort, or ease, or thing desirable on any account, if it stands in the way of this great concern, let it be dismissed without hesitation; and if it be of that nature that it is likely always to be a hindrance, then wholly have done with it, and never entertain any expectation from it more. If in time past you have, for the sake of worldly gain, involved yourself in more care and business than you find to be consistent with your being so thorough in the business of religion as you ought to be, then get into some other way, though you suffer in your worldly interest by it. Or if you have heretofore been conversant with company that you have reason to think have been and will be a snare to you, and a hindrance to this great design in any wise, break off from their

society, however it may expose you to reproach from your old companions, or let what will be the effect of it.

Whatever it be that stands in the way of your most advantageously seeking salvation—whether it be some dear sinful pleasure, or strong carnal appetite, or credit and honor, or the good-will of some persons whose friendship you desire, and whose esteem and liking you have highly valued—and though there be danger, if you do as you ought, that you shall looked upon by them as odd and ridiculous, and become contemptible in their eyes—or if it be your ease and indolence and aversion to continual labor; or your outward convenience in any respect, whereby you might avoid difficulties of one kind or other—let all go; offer up all such things together, as it were, in one sacrifice, to the interest of your soul. Let nothing stand in competition with this, but make everything to fall before it.

If the flesh must be crossed, then cross it, spare it not, crucify it, and do not be afraid of being too cruel to it. Galatians 5:24: "They that are Christ's have crucified the flesh, with the affections and lusts." Have no dependence on any worldly enjoyment whatsoever. Let salvation be the one thing with you. This is what is certainly required of you: and this is what many stick at; this giving up other things for salvation, is a stumbling-block that few get over.

While others pressed into the kingdom of God at the preaching of John the Baptist, Herod was pretty much stirred up by his preaching. It is said, he heard him, and observed him, and did many things; but when he came to tell him that he must part with his beloved Herodias, here he stuck; this he never would yield to, Mark 7:18–20.

The rich young man was considerably concerned for salvation; and accordingly was a very strict liver in many things: but when Christ came to direct him to go and sell all that he had, and give to the poor, and come and follow him, he could not find in his heart to comply with it, but went away sorrowful. He had great possessions, and set his heart much on his estate, and could not bear to part with it. It may be, if Christ had directed him only to give away a considerable part of his estate, he would have done it; yea, perhaps, if he had bid him part with half of it, he would have complied with it: but when he directed him to throw up all, he could not grapple with such a proposal.

Herein the straitness of the gate very much consists; and it is on this account that so many seek to enter in, and are not able. There are many that have a great mind to salvation, and spend great part of their time in wishing they had it, but they will not comply with the necessary means.

2. Be directed to forget the things that are behind: that is, not to keep thinking and making much of what you have done, but let your mind be wholly intent on what you have to do. In some sense you ought to look back; you should look back to your sins. Jeremiah 2:23: "See thy way in the valley, know what thou hast done."

You should look back on the wretchedness of your religious performances, and consider how you have fallen short in them; how exceedingly polluted all your duties have been, and how justly God might reject and loathe them, and you for them. But you ought not to spend your time in looking back, as many persons do, thinking how much they have done for their salvation; what great pains they have taken, how that they have done what they can, and do not see how they can do more; how long a time they have been seeking, and how much more they have done than others, and even than such and such who have obtained mercy. They think with themselves how hardly God deals with them, that he does not extend mercy to them, but turns a deaf ear to their cries; and hence discourage themselves, and complain of God.

Do not thus spend your time in looking back on what is past, but look forward, and consider what is before you; consider what it is that you can do, and what it is necessary that you should do, and what God calls you still to do, in order to your own salvation. The apostle, in the third chapter to the Philippians, tells us what things he did while a Jew, how much he had to boast of, if any could boast; but he tells us, that he forgot those things, and all other things that were behind, and reached forth towards the things that were before, pressing forwards towards the mark for the prize of the high calling of God in Christ Jesus.

3. Labor to get your heart thoroughly disposed to go on and hold out to the end. Many that seem to be earnest have not a heart thus disposed. It is a common thing for persons to appear greatly affected for a little while; but all is soon past away, and there is no more to be seen of it. Labor therefore to obtain a thorough willingness and preparation of spirit, to continue seeking, in the use of your utmost endeavors, without limitation; and do not think your whole life too long. And in order to this, be advised to two things,

First, remember that if ever God bestows mercy upon you, he will use his sovereign pleasure about the time when. He will bestow it on some in a little time, and on others not till they have sought it long. If other persons are soon enlightened and comforted, while you remain long in darkness, there is no other way but for you to wait. God will act arbitrarily in this matter, and you cannot help it. You must even be content to wait, in a way of laborious and earnest striving, till his time comes. If you refuse, you will but undo yourself; and when you shall hereafter find yourself undone, and see that your case is past remedy, how will you condemn yourself for foregoing a great probability of salvation, only because you had not the patience to hold out, and was not willing to be at the trouble of a persevering labor!

And what will it avail before God or your own conscience to say, that you could not bear to be obliged to seek salvation so long, when God bestowed it on others that sought it but for a very short time? Though God may have bestowed the testimonies of his favor on others in a few days or hours after they have begun earnestly to seek it, how does that alter the case as to you, if there proves to be a necessity of your laboriously seeking many years before you obtain them? Is salvation less worth taking a great deal of pains for, because, through the sovereign pleasure of God, others have obtained it with comparatively little pains?

If there are two persons, the one of which has obtained converting grace with comparative ease, and another that has obtained it after continuing for many years in the greatest and most earnest labors after it, how little difference does it make at last, when once salvation is obtained! Put all the labor and pains, the long-continued difficulties and strugglings, of the one in the scale against salvation, and how little does it subtract; and put the ease with which the other has obtained in the scale with salvation, and how little does it add! What is either added or subtracted is lighter than vanity, and a thing worthy of no consideration, when compared with that infinite benefit that is obtained. Indeed if you were [to wait] ten thousand years, and all that time should strive and press forward with as great earnestness as ever a person did for one day, all this would bear no proportion to the importance of the benefit; and it will doubtless appear little to you, when once you come to be in actual possession of eternal glory, and to see what that eternal misery is which you have escaped.

You must not think much of your pains, and of the length of time; you must press towards the kingdom of God, and do your utmost, and hold out to the end, and learn to make no account of it when you have done. You must undertake the business of seeking salvation upon these terms, and with no other expectations than this, that if ever God bestows mercy it will be in his own time; and not only so, but also that when you have done all, God will not hold himself obliged to show you mercy at last.

Secondly, endeavor now thoroughly to weigh in your mind the difficulty, and to count the cost of perseverance in seeking salvation. You that are now setting out in this business, (as there are many here who have very lately set about it—praised be the name of God that he has stirred you up to it!) be exhorted to attend this direction. Do not undertake in this affair with any other thought but of giving yourself wholly to it for the remaining part of your life, and going through many and great difficulties in it.

Take heed that you do not engage secretly upon this condition, that you shall obtain in a little time, promising yourself that it shall be within this present season of the pouring out of God's Spirit, or with any other limitation of time whatsoever. Many, when they begin, (seeming to set out very earnestly,) do not expect that they shall need to seek very long, and so do not prepare themselves for it. And therefore, when they come to find it otherwise, and meet with unexpected difficulty, they are found unguarded, and easily overthrown. But let me advise you all who are now seeking salvation, not to entertain any self-flattering thoughts; but weigh the utmost difficulties of perseverance, and be provided for them, having your mind fixed in it to go through them, let them be what they will.

Consider now beforehand, how tedious it would be, with utmost earnestness and labor, to strive after salvation for many years, in the mean time receiving no joyful or comfortable evidence of your having obtained. Consider what a great temptation to discouragement there probably would be in it; how apt you would be to yield the case; how ready to think that it is in vain for you to seek any longer, and that God never intends to show you mercy, in that he has not yet done it; how apt you would be to think with yourself,

> What an uncomfortable life do I live! How much more unpleasantly do I spend my time than others that do not perplex their minds about the things of another world, but are at ease, and take the comfort of their worldly enjoyments!

Consider what a temptation there would probably be in it, if you saw others brought in that began to seek the kingdom of heaven long after you, rejoicing in a hope and sense of God's favor, after but little pains and a short time of awakening; while you, from day to day, and from year to year, seemed to labor in vain. Prepare for such temptations now. Lay in beforehand for such trials and difficulties, that you may not think any strange thing has happened when they come.

I hope that those who have given attention to what has been said, have by this time conceived, in some measure, what is signified by the expression in the text, and after what manner they ought to press into the kingdom of God. Here is this to induce you to a compliance with what you have been directed to; if you sit still, you die; if you go backward, behold you shall surely die; if you go forward, you may live. And though God has not bound himself to anything that a person does while destitute of faith, and out of Christ, yet there is great probability, that in a way of hearkening to this counsel you will live; and that by pressing onward, and persevering, you will at last, as it were by violence, take the kingdom of heaven.

Those of you who have not only heard the directions given, but shall, through God's merciful assistance, practice according to them, are those that probably will overcome. These we may well hope at last to see standing with the Lamb on mount Zion, clothed in white robes, with palms in their hands; when all your labor and toil will be abundantly compensated, and you will not repent that you have taken so much pains, and denied yourself much, and waited so long. This self-denial, this waiting, will then look little, and vanish into nothing in your eyes, being all swallowed up in the first minute's enjoyment of that glory that you will then possess, and will uninterruptedly possess and enjoy to all eternity.

4. Improve the present season of the pouring out of the Spirit of God on this town. Prudence in any affair whatsoever consists very much in minding and improving our opportunities. If you would have spiritual prosperity, you must exercise prudence in the concerns of your souls, as well as in outward concerns when you seek outward prosperity. The prudent husbandman will observe his opportunities; he will improve seed-time and harvest; he will make his advantage of the showers and shines of heaven. The prudent merchant will discern his opportunities; he will not be idle on a market-day; he is careful not to let slip his seasons for enriching himself: So will those who prudently seek the fruits of righteousness, and the merchandise of wisdom, improve their opportunities for their eternal wealth and happiness.

God is pleased at this time, in a very remarkable manner, to pour out his Spirit amongst us (glory be to his name!). You that have a mind to obtain converting grace, and to go to heaven when you die, now is your season! Now, if you have any sort of prudence for your own salvation, and have not a mind to go to Hell, improve this season! Now is the accepted time! Now is the day of salvation! You that in time past have been called upon, and have turned a deaf ear to God's voice, and long stood out and resisted his commands and counsels, hear God's voice today, while it is called today! Do not harden your hearts at such a day as this! Now you have a special and remarkable price put into your hands to get wisdom, if you have but a heart to improve it.

God hath his certain days or appointed seasons of exercising both mercy and judgment. There are some remarkable times of wrath, laid out by God for his awful visitation, and the executions of his anger; which times are called days of vengeance, Proverbs 6:34. Wherein God will visit sin, Exodus 32:34. And so, on the contrary, God has laid out in his sovereign counsels seasons of remarkable mercy, wherein he will manifest himself in the exercises of his grace and loving-kindness, more than at other times. Such times in Scripture are called by way of eminency, accepted times, and days of salvation, and also days of God's visitation; because they are days wherein God will visit in a way of mercy; as in Luke 19:44.

> And shall lay thee even with the ground, and thy children within thee; and they shall not leave in thee one stone upon another; because thou knewest not the time of thy visitation.

It is such a time now in this town; it is with us a day of God's gracious visitation. It is indeed a day of grace with us as long as we live in this world, in the enjoyment of the means of grace; but such a time as this is especially, and in a distinguishing manner, a day of grace. There is a door of mercy always standing open for sinners; but such a day as this, God opens an extraordinary door.

We are directed to seek the Lord while he may be found, and to call upon him while he is near, Isaiah 55:6. If you that are hitherto Christless, be not strangely besotted and infatuated, you will by all means improve such an opportunity as this to get heaven, when heaven is brought so near, when the fountain is opened in the midst of us in so extraordinary a manner. Now is the time to obtain a supply of the necessities of your poor perishing souls! This is the day for sinners that have a mind to be converted before they die, when God is dealing forth so liberally and bountifully amongst us; when conversion and salvation work is going on amongst us from sabbath to sabbath, and many are pressing into the kingdom of God! Now do not stay behind, but press in amongst the rest! Others have been stirred up to be in good earnest, and have taken heaven by violence; be entreated to follow their example, if you would have a part of the inheritance with them, and would not be left at the great day, when they are taken!

How should it move you to consider that you have this opportunity now in your hands! You are in the actual possession of it! If it were past, it would not be in your power to recover it, or in the power of any creature to bring it back for you; but it is not past; it is now, at this day. Now is the accepted time, even while it is called today! Will you sit still at such a time? Will you sleep in such a harvest? Will you deal with a slack hand, and stay behind out of mere sloth, or love to some lust, or lothness to grapple with some small difficulty, or to put yourself a little out of your way, when so many are flowing to the goodness of the Lord? You are behind still; and so you will be in danger of being left behind, when the whole number is completed that are to enter in, if you do not earnestly bestir yourself! To be left behind at the close of such a season as this, will be awful—next to being left behind on that day when God's saints shall mount up as with wings to meet the Lord in the air—and will be what will appear [to be] very threatening of it [salvation].

God is now calling you in an extraordinary manner: and it is agreeable to the will and word of Christ, that I should now, in his name, call you, as one set over you, and sent to you to that end; so it is his will that you should hearken to what I say, as his voice. I therefore beseech you in Christ's stead now to press into the kingdom of God! Whoever you are, whether young or old, small or great; if you are a great sinner, if you have been a backslider, if you have quenched the Spirit, be who you will, do not stand making objections, but arise, apply yourself to your work! Do what you have to do with your might. Christ is calling you before, and holding forth his grace, and everlasting benefits, and wrath is pursuing you behind; wherefore fly for your life, and look not behind you!

But here I would particularly direct myself to several sorts of persons.

II. To those sinners who are in a measure awakened, and are concerned for their salvation.

You have reason to be glad that you have such an opportunity, and to prize it above gold. To induce you to prize and improve it, consider several things.

1. God has doubtless a design now to deal forth saving blessings to a number. God has done it to some already, and it is not probable that he has yet finished his work amongst us: we may well hope still to see others brought out of darkness into marvelous light.

And therefore,

2. God comes this day, and knocks at many persons' doors, and at your door among the rest. God seems to be come in a very unusual manner amongst us, upon a gracious and merciful design; a design of saving a number of poor miserable souls out of a lost and perishing condition, and of bringing them into a happy state and eternal glory! This is offered to you, not only as it has always been in the word and ordinances, but by the particular influences of the Spirit of Christ awakening you! This special offer is made to many amongst us; and you are not passed over. Christ has not forgot you; but has come to your door; and there, as it were, stands waiting for you to open to him. If you have wisdom and discretion to discern your own advantage, you will know that now is your opportunity.

3. How much more easily converting grace is obtained at such a time, than at other times! The work is equally easy with God at all times; but there is far less difficulty in the way as to men at such a time, than at other times. It is, as I said before, a day of God's gracious visitation; a day that he has, as it were, set apart for the more liberally and bountifully dispensing of his grace; a day wherein God's hand is opened wide. Experience shows it. God seems to be more ready to help, to give proper convictions, to help against temptations, and let in divine light. He seems to carry on his work with a more glorious discovery of his power, and Satan is more chained up than at other times. Those difficulties and temptations that persons before struck at, from year to year, they are soon helped over.

The work of God is carried on with greater speed and swiftness, and there are often instances of sudden conversion at such a time. So it was in the apostles' days, when there was a time of the most extraordinary pouring out of the Spirit that ever was. How quick and sudden were conversions in those days!

Such instances as that of the jailer abounded then, in fulfillment of that prophecy, Isaiah 66:7, 8:

> Before she travailed, she brought forth: before her pain came she was delivered of a man-child. Who hath heard such a thing? Who hath seen such things? For as soon as Zion travailed, she brought forth her children.

So it is in some degree, whenever there is an extraordinary pouring out of the Spirit of God; more or less so, in proportion to the greatness of that effusion. There is seldom such quick work made of it at other times. Persons are not so soon delivered from their various temptations and entanglements; but are much longer wandering in a wilderness, and groping in darkness. And yet,

4. *There are probably some here present that are now concerned about their salvation, that will never obtain.* It is not to be supposed that all that are now moved and awakened, will ever be savingly converted. Doubtless there are many now seeking that will not be able to enter. When has it been so in times past, when there has been times of great outpourings of God's Spirit, but that many who for a while have inquired with others, what they should do to be saved, have failed, and afterwards grown hard and secure? All of you that are now awakened, have a mind to obtain salvation, and probably hope to get a title to heaven, in the time of this present moving of God's Spirit: but yet, (though it be awful to be spoken, and awful to be thought) we have no reason to think any other, than that some of you will burn in Hell to all eternity.

You all are afraid of Hell, and seem at present disposed to take pains to be delivered from it; and yet it would be unreasonable to think any other, than that some of you will have your portion in the lake that burns with fire and brimstone. Though there are so many that seem to obtain so easily, having been but a little while under convictions, yet, for all that, some never will obtain. Some will soon lose the sense of things they now have; though their awakenings seem to be very considerable for the present, they will not hold; they have not hearts disposed to hold on through very many difficulties. Some that have set out for heaven, and hope as much as others to obtain, are indeed but slighty and slack, even now, in the midst of such a time as this. And others, who for the present seem to be more in earnest, will probably, before long, decline and fail, and gradually return to be as they were before. The convictions of some seem to be great, while that which is the occasion of their convictions is new; which, when that begins to grow old, will gradually decay and wear off.

Thus, it may be, the occasion of your awakening has been the hearing of the conversion of some person, or seeing so extraordinary a dispensation of Providence as this in which God now appears amongst us; but by and by the newness and freshness of these things will be gone, and so will not affect your mind as now they do; and it may be your convictions will go away with it.

Though this be a time wherein God doth more liberally bestow his grace, and so a time of greater advantage for obtaining it; yet there seems to be, upon some accounts, greater danger of backsliding, than when persons are awakened at other times. For commonly such extraordinary times do not last long; and then when they cease, there are multitudes that lose their convictions as it were together.

We speak of it as a happy thing, that God is pleased to cause such a time amongst us, and so it is indeed: but there are some to whom it will be no benefit; it will be an occasion of their greater misery; they will wish they had never seen this time; it will be more tolerable for those that never saw it, or anything like it, in the day of judgment, than for them. It is an awful consideration, that there are probably those here, whom the great Judge will hereafter call to a strict account about this very thing, why they no better improved this opportunity, when he set open the fountain of his grace, and so loudly called upon them, and came and strove with them in particular, by the awakening influences of his Spirit; and they will have no good account to give to the Judge, but their mouths will be stopped, and they will stand speechless before him.

You had need therefore to be earnest, and very resolved in this affair, that you may not be one of those who shall thus fail, that you may so fight, as not uncertainly, and so run, as that you may win the prize.

5. *Consider in what sad circumstances times of extraordinary effusion of God's Spirit commonly leave persons, when they leave them unconverted.* They find them in a doleful, because in a natural, condition; but commonly leave them in a much more doleful condition. They are left dreadfully hardened, and with a great increase of guilt, and their souls under a more strong dominion and possession of Satan. And frequently seasons of extraordinary advantage for salvation, when they pass over persons, and they do not improve them, nor receive any good in them, seal their damnation. As such seasons leave them, God forever leaves them, and gives them up to judicial hardness. Luke 19:41, 42:

> And when he was come near, he beheld the city, and wept over it, saying, If thou hadst known, even thou, the things which belong unto thy peace! but now they are hid from thine eyes.

6. *Consider, that it is very uncertain whether you will ever see such another time as this.* If there should be such another time, it is very uncertain whether you will live to another time, it is very uncertain whether you will eve whether you will live to see it. Many that are now concerned for their

salvation amongst us, will probably be in their graves, and it may be in Hell, before that time; and if you should miss this opportunity, it may be so with you. And what good will that do you, to have the Spirit of God poured out upon earth, in the place where you once lived, while you are tormented in Hell? What will it avail you, that others are crying, "What shall I do to be saved?" while you are shut up forever in the bottomless pit, and are wailing and gnashing your teeth in everlasting burnings?

Wherefore improve this opportunity, while God is pouring out his Spirit, and you are on earth, and while you dwell in the place where the Spirit of God is thus poured out, and you yourself have the awakening influences of it, that you may never wail and gnash your teeth in Hell, but may sing in heaven for ever, with others that are redeemed from amongst men, and redeemed amongst us.

7. *If you should see another such time, it will be under far greater disadvantages than now.* You will probably then be much older, and will have more hardened your heart; and so will be under less probability of receiving good. Some persons are so hardened in sin, and so left of God, that they can live through such a time as this, and not be much awakened or affected by it; they can stand their ground, and be but little moved. And so it may be with you, by another such time, if there should be another amongst us, and you should live to see it. The case in all probability will be greatly altered with you by that time.

If you should continue Christless and graceless till then, you will be much further from the kingdom of God, and much deeper involved in snares and misery; and the devil will probably have a vastly greater advantage against you, to tempt and confound you.

8. *We do not know but that God is now gathering in his elect, before some great and sore judgment.* It has been God's manner before he casts off a visible people, or brings some great and destroying judgments upon them, first to gather in his elect, that they may be secure. So it was before the casting off the Jews from being God's people. There was first a very remarkable pouring out of the Spirit, and gathering in of the elect, by the preaching of the apostles and evangelists, as we read in the beginning of the Acts: but after this the harvest and its gleanings were over, the rest were blinded, and hardened; the gospel had little success amongst them, and the nation was given up, and cast off from being God's people, and their city and land was destroyed by the Romans in a terrible manner; and they have been cast off by God now for a great many ages, and still remain a hardened and rejected

people. So we read in the beginning of the 7th chapter of the Revelations, that God, when about to bring destroying judgments on the earth, first sealed his servants in the forehead. He set his seal upon the hearts of the elect, gave them the saving influences and indwelling of his Spirit, by which they were sealed to the day of redemption. Revelation 7:1–3:

> And after these things, I saw four angels standing on the four corners of the earth, holding the four winds of the earth, that the wind should not blow on the earth, nor on the sea, nor on any tree. And I saw another angel ascending from the east, having the seal of the living God: and he cried with a loud voice to the four angels, to whom it was given to hurt the earth and the sea, saying, "Hurt not the earth, neither the sea, nor the trees, till we have sealed the servants of our God in their foreheads."

And this may be the case now, that God is about, in a great measure, to forsake this land, and give up this people, and to bring most awful and overwhelming judgments upon it, and that he is now gathering in his elect, to secure them from the calamity. The state of the nation, and of this land, never looked so threatening of such a thing as at this day. The present aspect of things exceedingly threatens vital religion, and even those truths that are especially the foundation of it, out of this land. If it should be so, how awful will the case be with those that shall be left, and not brought in, while God continues the influences of his Spirit, to gather in those that are to be redeemed from amongst us!

9. *If you neglect the present opportunity, and be finally unbelieving, those that are converted in this time of the pouring out of God's Spirit will rise up in judgment against you.* Your neighbors, your relations, acquaintance, or companions that are converted, will that day appear against you. They will not only be taken while you are left, mounting up with joy to meet the Lord in the air—at his right hand with glorious saints and angels, while you are at the left with devils—but how they will rise up in judgment against you.

However friendly you have been together, and have taken pleasure in one another's company, and have often familiarly conversed together, they will then surely appear against you. They will rise up as witnesses, and will declare what a precious opportunity you had, and did not improve; how you continued unbelieving, and rejected the offers of a Savior, when those offers were made in so extraordinary a manner, and when so many others were prevailed upon to accept of Christ; how you was negligent and slack, and did not know the things that belonged to your peace, in that your day.

And not only so, but they shall be your judges, as assessors with the great Judge; and as such will appear against you; they will be with the Judge in passing sentence upon you. 1 Corrinthians 6:2: "Know ye not that the saints shall judge the world?" Christ will admit them to the honor of judging the world with him: "They shall sit with him in his throne" (Revelation 3:21). They shall sit with Christ in his throne of government, and they shall sit with him in his throne of judgment, and shall be judges with him when you are judged, and as such shall condemn you.

10. *And lastly, you do not know that you shall live through the present time of the pouring out of God's Spirit.* You may be taken away in the midst of it, or you may be taken away in the beginning of it; as God in his providence is putting you in mind, by the late instance of death in a young person in the town.* God has of late been very awful in his dealings with us, in the repeated deaths of young persons amongst us. This should stir every one up to be in the more haste to press into the kingdom of God, that so you may be safe whenever death comes. This is a blessed season and opportunity; but you do not know how little of it you may have. You may have much less of it than others; may by death be suddenly snatched away from all advantages that are here enjoyed for the good of souls. Therefore make haste, and escape for thy life. One moment's delay is dangerous; for wrath is pursuing, and divine vengeance hanging over every uncovered person.

Let these considerations move every one to be improving this opportunity, that while others receive saving good, and are made heirs of eternal glory, you may not be left behind, in the same miserable doleful circumstances in which you came into the world, a poor captive to sin and Satan, a lost sheep, a perishing, undone creature, sinking down into everlasting perdition; that you may not be one of them spoken of in Jeremiah 17:6: ". . .that shall be like the heath in the desert, and shall not see when good comes." If you do not improve this opportunity, remember I have told you—you will hereafter lament it; and if you do not lament it in this world, then I will leave it with you to remember it throughout a miserable eternity.

II. I would address myself to such as yet remain unawakened.

It is an awful thing that there should be any one person remaining secure amongst us at such a time as this; but yet it is to be feared that there are some of this sort. I would here a little expostulate with such persons.

---

* Joseph Clark's wife, a young woman lately married, who died suddenly the week before this was delivered.

1. When do you expect that it will be more likely that you should be awakened and wrought upon than now? You are in a Christless condition; and yet without doubt intend to go to heaven; and therefore intend to be converted some time before you die; but this is not to be expected till you are first awakened, and deeply concerned about the welfare of your soul, and brought earnestly to seek God's converting grace. And when do you intend that this shall be? How do you lay things out in your own mind, or what projection have you about this matter? Is it ever so likely that a person will be awakened, as at such a time as this? How do we see many, who before were secure, now roused out of their sleep, and crying, "What shall I do to be saved?" But you are yet secure!

Do you flatter yourself that it will be more likely you should be awakened when it is a dull and dead time? Do you lay matters out thus in your own mind, that though you are senseless when others are generally awakened, that yet you shall be awakened when others are generally senseless? Or do you hope to see another such time of the pouring out of God's Spirit hereafter? And do you think it will be more likely that you should be wrought upon then, than now? And why do you think so? Is it because then you shall be so much older than you are now, and so that your heart will be grown softer and more tender with age? Or because you will then have stood out so much longer against the calls of the gospel, and all means of grace? Do you think it more likely that God will give you the needed influences of his Spirit then, than now, because then you will have provoked him so much more, and your sin and guilt will be so much greater? And do you think it will be any benefit to you, to stand it out through the present season of grace, as proof against the extraordinary means of awakening there are? Do you think that this will be a good preparation for a saving work of the Spirit hereafter?

2. What means do you expect to be awakened by? As to the awakening awful things of the word of God, you have had those set before you times without number, in the most moving manner that the dispensers of the word have been capable of. As to particular solemn warnings, directed to those that are in your circumstances, you have had them frequently, and have them now from time to time. Do you expect to be awakened by awful providences? Those also you have lately had, of the most awakening nature, one after another. Do you expect to be moved by the deaths of others? We have lately had repeated instances of these. There have been deaths of old and young: the year has been remarkable for the deaths of young persons in the bloom of life; and some of them very sudden deaths.

Will the conversion of others move you? There is indeed scarce any-thing that is found to have so great a tendency to stir persons up as this: and this you have been tried with of late in frequent instances; but are hitherto proof against it. Will a general pouring out of the Spirit, and see-ing a concern about salvation amongst all sorts of people, do it? This means you now have, but without effect. Yea, you have all these things together; you have the solemn warnings of God's word, and awful in-stances of death, and the conversion of others, and see a general concern about salvation: but all together do not move you to any great concern about your own precious, immortal, and miserable soul. Therefore con-sider by what means it is that you expect ever to be awakened.

You have heard that it is probable some who are now awakened, will never obtain salvation; how dark then does it look upon you that remain stupidly unawakened! Those who are not moved at such a time as this, come to adult age, have reason to fear whether they are not given up to judicial hardness. I do not say they have reason to conclude it, but they have reason to fear it. How dark doth it look upon you, that God comes and knocks at so many persons' doors, and misses yours! that God is giv-ing the strivings of his Spirit so generally amongst us, while you are left senseless!

3. *Do you expect to obtain salvation without ever seeking it?* If you are sen-sible that there is a necessity of your seeking in order to obtaining, and ever intend to seek, one would think you could not avoid it at such a time as this. Inquire therefore, whether you intend to go to heaven, living all your days a secure, negligent, careless life.

4. *Or, do you think you can bear the damnation of Hell?* Do you imagine that you can tolerably endure the devouring fire, and everlasting burn-ings? Do you hope that you shall be able to grapple with the vengeance of God Almighty, when he girds himself with strength, and clothes himself with wrath? Do you think to strengthen yourself against God, and to be able to make your part good with him? 1 Corrinthians 10:22: "Do we pro-voke the Lord to jealousy? Are we stronger than he?" Do you flatter your-self that you shall find out ways for your ease and support, and to make it out tolerably well, to bear up your spirit in those everlasting burnings that are prepared for the devil and his angels? Ezekiel 22:14. "Can thine heart endure, or can thine hands be strong, in the days that I shall deal with thee?" It is a difficult thing to conceive what such Christless persons think, that are unconcerned at such a time.

III. I would direct myself to them who are grown considerably into years, and are yet in a natural condition.

I would now take occasion earnestly to exhort you to improve this extraordinary opportunity, and press into the kingdom of God. You have lost many advantages that once you had, and now have not the same advantages that others have. The case is very different with you from what it is with many of your neighbors. You, above all, had need to improve such an opportunity. Now is the time for you to bestir yourself, and take the kingdom of heaven! Consider:

1. *Now there seems to be a door opened for old sinners.* Now God is dealing forth freely to all sorts: his hand is opened wide, and he does not pass by old ones so much as he used to do. You are not under such advantages as others who are younger; but yet, so wonderfully has God ordered it, that now you are not destitute of great advantage. Though old in sin, God has put a new and extraordinary advantage in your hands. O! improve [put to good use] this price you have to get wisdom. You that have been long seeking to enter in at the strait gate and yet remain without, now take your opportunity and press in! You that have been long in the wilderness, fighting with various temptations, laboring under discouragements, ready to give up the case, and have been often tempted to despair, now, behold the door that God opens for you!

Do not give way to discouragements now; this is not a time for it. Do not spend time in thinking, that you have done what you can already, and that you are not elected, and in giving way to other perplexing, weakening, disheartening temptations. Do not waste away this precious opportunity in such a manner. You have no time to spare for such things as these; God calls you now to something else. Improve this time in seeking and striving for salvation, and not in that which tends to hinder it. It is no time now for you to stand talking with the devil; but hearken to God, and apply yourself to that which he does now so loudly call you to.

Some of you have often lamented the loss of past opportunities, particularly, the loss of the time of youth, and have been wishing that you had so good an opportunity again; and have been ready to say, "O! If I was young again, how would I improve such an advantage!" That opportunity which you have had in time past is irrecoverable; you can never have it again; but God can give you other advantages of another sort, that are very great, and he is so doing at this day. He is now putting a new opportunity into your hands; though not of the same kind with that which you once had, and have lost, yet in some respects as great of another kind. If you lament your folly in neglecting and losing past opportunities, then do not be guilty of the folly of neglecting the opportunity which God now gives you. This opportunity you could not have purchased, if you would have given all that you had in the world for it. But God is putting it into your hands himself, of his own free and sovereign mercy, without your purchasing it. Therefore when you have it, do not neglect it.

2. *It is a great deal more likely with respect to such persons than others, that this is their last time.* There will be a last time of special offer of salvation to impenitent sinners: "God's Spirit shall not always strive with man," Genesis 6:3. God sometimes continues long knocking at the doors of wicked men's hearts; but there are the last knocks, and the last calls that ever they shall have. And sometimes God's last calls are the loudest; and then if sinners do not hearken, he finally leaves them. How long has God been knocking at many of your doors that are old in sin! It is a great deal more likely that these are his last knocks. You have resisted God's Spirit in times past, and have hardened your heart once and again; but God will not be thus dealt with always. There is danger, that if now, after so long a time, you will not hearken, he will utterly desert you, and leave you to walk in your own counsels.

It seems by God's providence, as though God had yet an elect number amongst old sinners in this place, that perhaps he is now about to bring in. It looks as though there were some that long lived under Mr. Stoddard's ministry, that God has not utterly cast off, though they stood it out under such great means as they then enjoyed. It is to be hoped that God will now bring in a remnant from among them. But it is more likely that God is now about finishing with them, one way or other, for their having been so long the subjects of such extraordinary means.

You have seen former times of the pouring out of God's Spirit upon the town, when others were taken and you left, others were called out of darkness into marvelous light, and were brought into a glorious and happy state, and you saw not good when good came. How dark will your circumstances appear, if you shall also stand it out through this opportunity, and still be left behind! Take heed that you be not of those spoken of in Hebrews 6:7, 8, that are like the "earth that has rain coming oft upon it, and only bears briers and thorns." As we see, there are some pieces of ground, the more showers of rain fall upon them, the more fruitful seasons there are, the more do the briers, and other useless and hurtful plants, that are rooted in them, grow and flourish. Of such ground the apostle says, "It is rejected, and is nigh unto cursing, whose end is to be burned."

The way that the husbandman takes with such ground, is, to set fire to it, to burn up the growth of it. If you miss this opportunity, there is danger that you will be utterly rejected, and that your end will be to be burned. And if this is to be, it is to be feared, that you are not far from, but nigh unto, cursing.

Those of you that are already grown old in sin, and are now under awakenings, when you feel your convictions begin to go off, if ever that should be, then remember what you have now been told; it may well then strike you to the heart!

IV. I would direct the advice to those that are young, and now under their first special convictions.

I would earnestly urge such to improve this opportunity, and press into the kingdom of God. Consider two things,

1. *You have all manner of advantages now centering upon you.* It is a time of great advantage for all; but your advantages are above others. There is no other sort of persons that have now so great and happy an opportunity as you have. You have the great advantage that is common to all who live in this place, viz. that now it is a time of the extraordinary pouring out of the Spirit of God. And have you not that great advantage, the awakening influences of the Spirit of God on you in particular? and besides, you have this peculiar advantage, that you are now in your youth. And added to this, you have another unspeakable advantage, that you now are under your first convictions. Happy is he that never has hardened his heart, and blocked up his own way to heaven by backsliding, and has now the awakening influences of God's Spirit, if God does but enable him thoroughly to improve them! Such above all in the world bid fair for the kingdom of God. God is wont on such, above any kind of persons, as it were easily and readily to bestow the saving grace and comforts of his Spirit. Instances of speedy and sudden conversion are most commonly found among such. Happy are they that have the Spirit of God with them, and never have quenched it, if they did but know the price they have in their hands!

If you have a sense of your necessity of salvation, and the great worth and value of it, you will be willing to take the surest way to it, or that which has the greatest probability of success; and that certainly is, thoroughly to improve your first convictions. If you so go, it is not likely that you will fail; there is the greatest probability that you will succeed. What is it not worth, to have such an advantage in one's hands for obtaining eternal life? The present season of the pouring out of God's Spirit, is the first that many of you who are now under awakenings have ever seen, since you came to years of understanding. On which account, it is the greatest opportunity that ever you had, and probably by far the greatest that ever you will have. There are many here present who wish they had such an opportunity, but they never can obtain it; they cannot buy it for money; but you have it in your possession, and can improve it if you will. But yet,

2. *There is on some accounts greater danger that such as are in your circumstances will fail of thoroughly improving their convictions, with respect to steadfastness and perseverance, than others.* Those that are young are more unstable than elder persons. They who never had convictions before, have less experience of the difficulty of the work they have engaged in; they are more ready to think that they shall obtain salvation easily, and are more easily discouraged by disappointments; and young persons have less reason and consideration to fortify them against temptations to backsliding. You should therefore labor now the more to guard against such temptations. By all means make but one work of seeking salvation! Make thorough work of it the first time! There are vast disadvantages that they bring themselves under, who have several turns of seeking with great intermissions. By such a course, persons exceedingly wound their own souls, and entangle themselves in many snares. Who are those that commonly meet with so many difficulties, and are so long laboring in darkness and perplexity, but those who have had several turns at seeking salvation; who have, [for] one while, had convictions, and then have quenched them, and then have set about the work again, and have backslidden again, and have gone on after that manner?

The children of Israel would not have been forty years in the wilderness, if they had held their courage, and had gone on as they set out; but they were of an unstable mind, and were for going back again into Egypt. Otherwise, if they had gone right forward without discouragement, as God would have led them, they would have soon entered and taken possession of Canaan. They had got to the very borders of it when they turned back, but were thirty-eight years after that, before they got through the wilderness. Therefore, as you regard the interest of your soul, do not run yourself into a like difficulty, by unsteadiness, intermission, and backsliding; but press right forward, from henceforth, and make but one work of seeking, converting, and pardoning grace, however great, and difficult, and long a work that may be.

The Character of Paul an Example to Christians

Dated February 1739/1740. Originally four sermons.

"Brethren, be followers of me, and mark them which walk so as ye have us for an example."—Philippians 3:17

The apostle, in the foregoing part of the chapter, had been telling how he counted all things but loss for the excellency of the knowledge of Christ Jesus, and in the text he urges that his example should be followed.

He does this in two ways.

- He exhorts the Philippian Christians to follow his example. "Brethren, be followers together of me." He exhorts them to be followers of him *together*; that is, that they should all follow his example with one heart and soul, agreeing in it, and that all, as much as in them lay, should help and assist each other in it.

- That they should take particular notice of others that did so, and put peculiar honor on them, which is implied in the expression in the latter part of the verse, "mark them which walk so as ye have us for an example."

Doctrine

We ought to follow the good examples of the apostle Paul. We are to consider that the apostle did not say this of himself from an ambitious spirit, from a desire of being set up as a pattern, and eyed and imitated as an example to other Christians. His writings are not of any private interpretation, but he spoke as he was moved by the Holy Ghost. The Holy Ghost directed that the good examples of the apostle Paul should be noticed by other Christians and imitated. And we are also to consider that this is not a command to the Philippians only, to whom the epistle was more immediately directed, but to all those for whose use this epistle was written—for all Christians to the end of the world. For though God so ordered it, that the epistles of the apostles were mostly written on particular occasions and directed to particular churches, yet they were written to be of universal use. And those occasions were so ordered in the wisdom of Divine Providence that they are a part of that infallible rule of faith and manners which God has given to the Christian church to be their rule in all ages. And the precepts that we find in those epistles are no more to be regarded as precepts intended only for those to whom the epistle was sent, than the ten commandments that were spoken from mount Sinai to the children of Israel are to be regarded as commands intended only for that people.

And when we are directed to follow the good examples of the apostle Paul by the Holy Ghost, it is not merely as we are to imitate whatever we see that is good in anyone, let him be how he may. But there are spiritual obligations that lie on Christians to follow the good examples of this great apostle. And it has pleased the Holy Ghost in an especial manner to set up the apostle Paul, not only as a teacher of the Christian church, but as a patter to other Christians.

The greatest example of all, that is set before us in Scripture to imitate, is the example of Jesus Christ, which he set us in his human nature, and when in his state of humiliation. This is presented to us not only as a great pattern, but as a perfect rule. And the example of no man is set forth, as our rule, but the example of Christ. We are commanded to follow the examples which God himself set us, or the acts of the divine nature. Eph. 5:1, "Be ye therefore followers of God , as dear children." And Mat. 5:48, "Be ye therefore perfect, even as your Father which is in heaven is perfect." But the example of Christ Jesus, when on earth, is more especially our pattern. For though the acts of the divine nature have the highest possible perfection, and though his inimitable perfection is our best example, yet God is so much above us, his nature is infinitely different from ours, that it is not possible that his acts should be so accommodated to our nature and circumstances, as to be an example of so great and general use, as the perfect example in our nature which Christ has set us.

Christ, though a divine person, was man, as we are men. And not only so, but he was, in many respects, a partaker of our circumstances. He dwelt among men. He depended on food and raiment, and such outward supports of life, as we do. He was subject to the changes of time, and the afflictions and calamities of this evil world, and to abuse from men's corruptions, and to temptations from Satan, as we are; was subject to the same law and rule that we are, sued the same ordinances, and had many of our trials, and greater trials than we. So that Christ's example is the example that is chiefly offered in Scripture for our imitation.

But yet the example of some that are fallen creatures, as we are, may in some respects be more accommodated to our circumstances, and more fitted for our instructions, than the example of Jesus Christ. For though he became man as we are, and was like us, and was in our circumstances in so many respects, yet in other things there was a vast difference. He was the head of the church, and we are the members. He is Lord of all, we are his subjects and disciples. And we need an example, that shall teach and direct us how to behave towards Christ our Lord and head. And this we may have better in some, that have Christ for their Lord as well as we, than in Christ himself. But the greatest difference lies in this, that Christ had no sin, and we all are sinful creatures, all carry about with us a body of sin and death. It is said that Christ was made like to us in all things, sin only excepted. But this *was* excepted, and therefore there were many things required of us, of which Christ could not give us an example—such as repentance for sin, brokenness of spirit of sin, mortification of lust, warring against sin. And the excellent example of some, that are naturally as sinful as well, has this advantage, that we may regard it as the example of those who were naturally every way in our circumstances, and labored under the same natural difficulties, and the same opposition of heart to that which is good, as ourselves; which tends to engage us to give more heed to their example, and the more to encourage and animate us to strive to follow it.

And therefore we find that the Scripture does not only recommend the example of Christ, but does also exhibit some mere men, that are of like passions with ourselves, as patterns for us to follow. So it exhibits the eminent saints of the Old Testament, of whom we read in the Scripture, that they inherit the promises. Heb. 6:12, "That ye be not slothful, but followers of them who through faith and patience inherit the promises." In the eleventh chapter of Hebrews, a great number of eminent saints are mentioned as patterns for us to follow. Abraham is, in a particular manner, set forth as an example of his faith, and as the pattern of believers. Rom. 4:12:

> "And the father of circumcision to them, that are not of the circumcision only, but who also walk in the steps of that faith of our father Abraham, which he had, being yet uncircumcised."

And so the prophets of the Old Testament are also recommended as patterns. James 5:10: "Take, my brethren, the prophets, who have spoken in the name of the Lord, for an example of suffering affliction, and of patience." And so, eminently holy men under the New Testament, apostles and others, that God sent forth to preach the gospel, are also examples for Christians to follow. Heb. 13:7, "Remember them that have the rule over you, who have spoken to you the Word of God; whose faith follow, considering the end of their conversation." But of all mere men, no one is so often particularly set forth in the Scripture as a pattern for Christians to follow, as the apostle Paul. Our observing his holy conversation as our example is not only insisted on in the text, but also 1 Cor. 4:16, "Wherefore I beseech you, be followers of me." And chap. 11:1, "Be ye followers of me as I also am of Christ." And 1 Thes. 1:6, where the apostle commends the Christian Thessalonians for imitating his example; "and ye became followers of us." In 2 Thes. 3:7, he insists on this as their duty, "For yourselves know how ye ought to follow us."

For the more full treatment of this subject

> I. I shall, particularly mention many of the good examples of the apostle Paul that we ought to imitate, which I shall treat of not merely as a doctrine, but also in the way of application.
>
> II. I shall show under what strict obligation we are to follow the good examples of this apostle.

I. I shall particularly mention many of those good examples of the apostle Paul that we ought to imitate. And that I may be more distinct, I shall,

> *First,* mention those things that respect his watchfulness for the good of his own soul.
>
> *Secondly,* mention those virtues in him that more immediately respected God and Christ.

Third, those that more immediately respect men.

Fourth, those that were exercised in his behavior, both towards God and men.

1. *We ought to follow the good example that the apostle Paul has set us in his seeking the good of his own soul.*

First, we should follow him in his earnestness in seeking his own salvation. He was not careless and indifferent in this matter; but the kingdom of heaven suffered violence from him. He did not halt between two opinions, or seek with a wavering, unsteady mind, but with the most full determination and strong resolution. He resolved, if it could by any means be possible, that he would attain to the resurrection of the dead.

He does not say that he was determined to attain it, if he could, by means that were not very costly or difficult, or by laboring for it a little time, or only now and then, or without any great degree of suffering, or without great loss in his temporal interest. But if by *any* means he could do it, he would, let the means be easy or difficult. Let it be a short labor and trial, or a long one; let the cross be light or heavy; it was all one to his resolution. Let the requisite means be what they would, if it were possible, he would obtain it. He did not hesitate at worldly losses, for he tells us that he readily suffered the loss of all things, that he might win Christ, and be found in him, and in his righteousness. (Phil. 3:8, 9.)

It was not with him as it was with the young man, that came kneeling to Christ to inquire of him what he should do to inherit eternal life, and when Christ said, "Go and sell all that thou hast and give to the poor," he went away sorrowful. He was not willing to part with *all.* If Christ had bid him sell half, it may be, he would have complied with it. He had a great desire to secure salvation.

But the apostle Paul did not content himself with wishing. He was resolved, if it were possible, that he would obtain it. And when it was needful that he should lose worldly good, or when any great suffering was in his way, it was no cause of hesitation to him. He had been in very comfortable and honorable circumstances among the Jews. He had received the best education that was to be had among them, being brought up at the feet of Gamaliel, and was regarded as a very learned young man. His own nation, the Jews, had a high esteem of him, and he was esteemed for his moral and religious qualifications among them.

But when he could not hold the outward benefit of these things and win Christ, he despised them totally, he parted with all his credit and honor. He made nothing of them, that he might win Christ. And instead of being honored and loved, and living in credit, as before among his own nation, he made himself the object of their universal hatred. He lost all, and the Jews hated him, and persecuted him everywhere. And when great sufferings were in the way, he willingly made himself conformable to Christ's death, that he might have a part in his resurrection. He parted with his honor, his ease, his former friends and former acquaintances, his worldly goods and everything else, and plunged himself into a state of extreme labor, contempt, and suffering. And in this way he sought the kingdom of heaven.

He acted in this matter very much as one that is running a race for some great prize, who makes running his great and only business, till he has reached the end of the race, and strains every nerve and sinew, and suffers nothing to divert him, and will not stand to listen to what anyone says to him, but presses forward. Or as a man that is engaged in battle, sword in hand, with strong and violent enemies, that seek his life, who exerts himself to his utmost, as for his life. 1 Cor. 9:26, "I therefore so run, not as uncertainly; so fight I, not as one that beateth the air."

When fleshly appetites stood in the way, however importunate they were, he utterly denied them and renounced them. They were no impediment in the way of his thorough pursuit of salvation. He would not be subject to the appetites of his body, but made them subject to his soul. 1 Cor. 9:27, "I keep under my body, and bring it into subjection." Probably there never was a soldier, when he bore his part in storming a city, that acted with greater resolution and violence, as it were forcing his way through all that opposed him, than the apostle Paul in seeking the kingdom of heaven. We have not only his own word for it; the history we have of his life, written by St. Luke, shows the same.

Now those who seek their salvation ought to follow this example. Persons who are concerned for their salvation, sometimes inquire what they shall do. Let them do as did the apostle Paul, seek salvation in the way he did, with the like violence and resolution. Those that make this inquiry, who are somewhat anxious year after year, and complain that they have not obtained any comfort, would do well to ask themselves whether they seek salvation in any measure in this way, with that resolution and violence of which he set them an example. Alas, are they not very far indeed from it? Can it in any proper sense be said, that the kingdom of heaven suffers violence at their hands?

Secondly, the apostle did not only thus earnestly seek salvation before his conversion and hope, but afterwards also. What he says in the third chapter of Philippians of his suffering the loss of all things, that he might be found in Christ, and its being the one thing that he did to seek salvation; and also what he says of his so running as not in vain, but as resolving to win the prize of salvation, and keeping under his body that he might not be a castaway—were long after his conviction, and after he had renounced all hope of his own good estate by nature. If being a convinced sinner excuses a man from seeking salvation any more, or makes it reasonable that he should cease his earnest care and labor for it, certainly the apostle might have been excused, when he had not only already attained true grace, but such eminent degrees of it. To see one of the most eminent saints that ever lived, if not the most eminent of all, so exceedingly engaged in seeking his own salvation, ought forever to put to shame those who are a thousand degrees below him, and are but mere infants to him, if they have any grace at all, who yet excuse themselves from using any violence after the kingdom of heaven now because they have attained already, who free themselves from the burden of going on earnestly to seek salvation with this, that they have finished the work, they have obtained a hope.

The apostle, as eminent as he was, did not say within himself:

> I am converted, and so am sure of salvation. Christ has promised it me. Why need I labor any more to secure it? Yea, I am not only converted, but I have obtained great degrees of grace.

But still he is violent after salvation. He did not keep looking back on the extraordinary discoveries he enjoyed at his first conversion, and the past great experience he had had from time to time. He did not content himself with the thought that he possessed the most wonderful testimonies of God's favor, and of the love of Christ, already, that ever any enjoyed, even to his being caught up to the third heavens. But he forgot the things that were behind. He acted as though he did not consider that he had yet attained an interest in Christ. Phil. 3:11–14,

> If by any means I might attain unto the resurrection of the dead; not as though I had already attained, either [or] were already perfect; but I follow after, if that I may apprehend that for which I am apprehended of Christ Jesus. Brethren, I count not myself to have apprehended; but this one thing I do, forgetting those things which are behind, and reaching forth to those things which are before. I press toward the mark for the prize of the high calling of God in Christ Jesus.

The apostle still sought that he might win Christ and his righteousness, and attain to his resurrection, not as though he had attained it already, or had already obtained a title to the crown. And this is especially the thing in which he calls on us to imitate his example in the text. It was not because Paul was at a loss whether he was truly converted or not, that he was still so earnest in seeking salvation. He not only thought that he was converted, and should go to heaven when he died, but he knew and spoke particularly about it in this very epistle, in the twenty-first verse of the first chapter (Phil. 1:21), "For me to live is Christ, but to die is gain." And in the foregoing verse he says, "According to my earnest expectation and my hope that in nothing I shall be ashamed, but that with all boldness, as always, so now also Christ shall be magnified in my body, whether it be by life or by death." The apostle knew that though he was converted, yet there remained a great work that he must do in order to his salvation. There was a narrow way to eternal glory, through which he must pass, and never could come to heaven in any other way. He knew it was absolutely necessary for him earnestly to seek salvation still. He knew there was no going to heaven in a slothful way. And therefore he did not seek salvation the less earnestly, for his having hope and assurance, but a great deal more. We nowhere read so much of his earnestness and violence for the kingdom of heaven before he was converted, as afterwards. The apostle's hope was not of a nature to make him slothful. It had a contrary effect. The assurance he had of victory, together with the necessity there was of fighting, engaged him to fight not as one that beat the air, but as one that wrestled with principalities and powers.

Now this example the apostle does especially insist in the text that we ought to follow. And this should induce all present who think themselves converted, to inquire whether they seek salvation never the less earnestly, because they think it is well with them, and that they are now sure of heaven. Most certainly if the apostle was in the right way of acting, we in this place are generally in the wrong. For nothing is more apparent than that it is not thus with the generality of professors here, but that it is a common thing after they think they are safe, to be far less diligent and earnest in religion than before.

Third, the apostle did not only diligently seek heaven after he knew he was converted, but was earnestly cautious lest he should be damned, as appears by the passage already cited. "But I keep under my body and bring it into subjection, lest by any means, when I have preached to others, I myself should be a castaway." Here you see the apostle is very careful lest he should be a castaway, and denies his carnal appetites, and mortifies his flesh, for that reason. He did not say, "I am safe, I am sure I shall never be lost; why need I take any further care respecting it?" Many think because they suppose themselves converted, and so safe, that they have nothing to do with the awful threatenings of God's Word, and those terrible denunciations of damnation that are contained in it. When they hear them, they hear them as things which belong only to others, and not at all to themselves, as though there were no application of what is revealed in the Scripture respecting Hell, to the godly. And therefore, when they hear awakening sermons about the awful things that God has threatened to the wicked, they do not hear them for themselves, but only for others.

But it was not thus with this holy apostle, who certainly was as safe from Hell, and as far from a damnable state, as any of us. He looked upon himself as still nearly concerned in God's threatenings of eternal damnation, notwithstanding all his hope, and all his eminent holiness, and therefore gave great diligence, that he might avoid eternal damnation. For he considered that eternal misery was as certainly connected with a wicked life as ever it was, and that it was absolutely necessary that he should still keep under his body, and bring it into subjection, in order that he might not be damned, because indulging the lusts of the body and being damned were more surely connected together. The apostle knew that this conditional proposition was true concerning him, as ever it was. "If I live wickedly, or do not live in a way of universal obedience to God's commands, I shall certainly be a castaway." This is evident because the apostle mentions a proposition of this nature concerning himself in that very chapter where he says, he kept under his body lest he should be a castaway. 1 Cor. 9:16, "For though I preach the gospel, I have nothing to glory of, for necessity is laid upon me; yea, woe is unto me if I preach not the gospel."

What necessity was there upon the apostle to preach the gospel, though God had commanded him, for he was already converted, and was safe? And if he had neglected to preach the gospel, how could he have perished after he was converted? But yet this conditional proposition was still true. If he did not live a life of obedience to God, woe would be to him; woe to him, if he did not preach the gospel. The connection still held. It is impossible a man should go anywhere else than to Hell in a way of disobedience to God. And therefore he deemed it necessary for him to preach the gospel on that account, and on the same account he deemed it necessary to keep under his body, lest he should be a castaway.

The connection between a wicked life and damnation is so certain, that if a man lives a wicked life, it proves that all his supposed experiences are nothing. If a man at the last day be found a worker of iniquity, nothing else will be inquired of about him. Let him pretend what he will, Christ will say to him and all others like him, "Depart from me, I know you not, ye that work iniquity." And God has revealed these threatenings and this connection, not only to deter wicked men, but also godly men, from sin. And though God will keep men that are converted from damnation, yet this is the means by which he will keep them from it; viz. he will keep them from a wicked life. And though he will keep them from a wicked life, yet this is one means by which he will keep them from it, viz. by their own caution to avoid damnation, and by his threatenings of damnation if they should live a wicked life.

We have another remarkable instance in Job, who was an eminently holy man, yet avoided sin with the utmost care, because he would avoid destruction from God. (Job 31.) Surely we have as much cause to be cautious, that we do not expose ourselves to destruction from God, as holy Job had. We have not a greater stock of goodness than he. The apostle directs Christians to work out their own salvation with fear and trembling. (Phil. 2:12.) And it is spoken of as the character of a true saint, that he trembles at God's Word; (Isa. 66:2), which is to tremble especially at the awful threatenings of it, as Job did. Whereas the manner of many now is, whenever they think they are converted, to throw by those threatenings of God's Word, as if they had no more to do with them, because they suppose they are converted, and out of danger. Christ gave his disciples, even those of them that were converted, as well as others, directions to strive for salvation because broad was the way that leads to destruction, and men are so apt to walk in that way and be damned. Matt. 7:13, 14:

> Enter ye in at the strait gate; for wide is the gate, and broad is the way, that leadeth to destruction, and many there be which go in thereat; because strait is the gate, and narrow is the way, which leadeth unto life, and few there be that find it."

Fourth, the apostle did not seek salvation by his own righteousness. Though his sufferings were so very great, his labors so exceedingly abundant, yet he never accounted them as righteousness. He trod it [righteousness] under his feet, as utterly insufficient to recommend him to God. He gave diligence that he might be found in Christ, not having on his own righteousness, which is of God, through faith, as in the foregoing part of the chapter from which the text is taken, beginning with the fourth verse (Phil. 3:4),

> Though I might also have confidence in the flesh. If any other man thinketh he hath whereof he might trust in the flesh, I more; circumcised the eighth day, of the stock of Israel, of the tribe of Benjamin, a Hebrew of the Hebrews; as touching the law, a Pharisee; concerning zeal, persecuting the church; touching the righteousness which is in the law, blameless. But what things were gain to me, those I counted loss for Christ. Yea, doubtless, and I count all things but loss for the excellency of the knowledge of Christ Jesus, my Lord; for whom I have suffered the loss of all things, and do count them but dung, that I may win Christ, and be found in him, not having on mine own righteousness, which is of the law, but that which is through the faith of Christ, the righteousness which is of God by faith; that I may know him, and the power of his resurrection, and the fellowship of his sufferings, being made conformable unto his death; if by any means I might attain unto the resurrection of the dead. Not as though I had already attained, either were already perfect; but I follow after, if that I may apprehend that for which also I am apprehended of Christ Jesus.

Fifth, in those earnest labors which he performed, he had respect to the recompense of the reward. He did it for an incorruptible crown. (1 Cor 9:25.) He sought a high degree of glory, for he knew the more he labored the more he should be rewarded, as appears from what he tells the Corinthians. "He that soweth sparingly, shall reap also sparingly; and he that soweth bountifully, shall reap also bountifully." And 1 Cor. 3:8, "Every man shall receive his own reward, according to his own labor." That he had respect to that crown of glory, which is Master had promised, in those great labors and sufferings, is evident from what he says to Timothy, a little before his death. 2 Tim. 4:7, 8:

> I have fought a good fight, I have finished my course, I have kept the faith; henceforth there is laid up for me a crown of righteousness, which the Lord, the righteous Judge, shall give me at that day; and not to me only, but unto all them also that love his appearing.

All Christians should follow his example in this also. They should not content themselves with the thought that they have goodness enough to carry them to heaven, but should earnestly seek high degrees of glory. For the higher degrees of glory are promised to extraordinary labors for God, for no other reason, but that we should seek them.

2. I proceed to mention some of the virtues of Paul, that more immediately re-spect God and Christ, in which we ought to follow his example.

First, he was strong in faith. It may be truly said of him that he lived by faith. His faith seemed to be even without the least appearance of diffidence or doubt in his words or actions, but all seemed to proclaim, that he had God and Christ and the invisible world continually in view. Such a faith, that was in continual exercise in him, he professes in 2 Cor. 5:6–8:

> Therefore we are always confident, knowing that while we are at home in the body, we are absent from the Lord. For we walk by faith, not by sight. We are confident, I say, and willing rather to be absent from the body, and to be present with the Lord.

He always speaks of God and Christ and things invisible and future, as if he certainly knew them, and then saw them as fully and certainly as we see anything that is immediately before our bodily eyes. He spoke as though he certainly knew that God's promise of eternal life should be accomplished, and gives this as the reason why he labored so abundantly, and endured all manner of temporal sufferings and death, and was always delivered unto death for Christ's sake. 2 Cor. 4:11, etc. "For we which live are always delivered unto death for Jesus' sake, that the life also of Jesus might be made manifest in our mortal flesh." He speaks of his earnest expectation and hope of the fulfillment of God's promises. And a little before his death, when he was a prisoner, and when he knew that he was like [likely] to bear the trial of martyrdom, which is the greatest trial of faith, he expresses his faith in Christ in the strongest terms. 2 Tim. 1:12:

> For the which cause I also suffer these things; nevertheless I am not ashamed, for I know whom I have believed, and am persuaded that he is able to keep that which I have committed unto him against that day.

Such an example may well make us ashamed; for how weak and unsteady is the faith of most Christians! If now and then there seems to be a lively exercise of faith, giving the person at that time a firm persuasion and confidence; yet how short are such exercises, how soon do they vanish! How often is faith shaken with one temptation. How often are the exercises of it interrupted with doubting, and how much is exhibited of a diffident, vibrating spirit! How little does our faith accomplish in times of trial. How often and how easily is our confidence in God shaken and interrupted, and how frequently does unbelief prevail! This is much to the dishonor of our Savior Jesus Christ, as well as very painful to us. What a happy and glorious lot it is to live such a life of faith, as Paul lived! How far did he soar on the wings of his strong faith above those little difficulties, that continually molest us, and are ready to overcome us! Seeing we have such a blessed example set before us in the Scriptures, let it prompt us earnestly to seek, that we may soar higher also.

Secondly, another virtue in which we should follow his example is his great love to Christ. The Corinthians, who saw how the apostle acted, how he labored, and how he suffered, and could see no worldly motive, were astonished. They wondered what it was that so wonderfully influenced and actuated the man. The apostle says that he was a spectacle to the world. But this was the immediate principle that moved him: his strong, his intense love to his glorious Lord and Master. This love constrained him, that he could do nothing else than strive and labor and seek for his salvation. This account he gives of it himself. 2 Cor. 5:14, "The love of Christ constraineth us."

He had such a delight in the Lord Jesus Christ, and in the knowledge and contemplation of him, that he tells us, he "counted all things but loss for the excellency of the knowledge of Christ Jesus." He speaks in very positive terms. He does not say merely that he hopes he loves Christ, so as to despise other things in comparison of the knowledge of him. But "yea, doubtless, I count all things but loss for the excellency of the knowledge of Christ Jesus, my Lord." And he assigns this reason why he even gloried in his sufferings for Christ's sake, because the love of God was shed abroad in his heart, by the Holy Ghost. (Rom. 5:5.) This expression seems to imply that he sensibly felt that holy affection, sweetly and powerfully diffused in his soul, like some precious, fragrant ointment. And how does he triumph in his love to Christ in the midst of his sufferings! Rom. 8:35–37:

> Who shall separate us from the love of Christ? Shall tribulation, or distress, or persecution, or famine, or nakedness, or peril, or sword? As it is written, For thy sake we are killed all the day long; we are accounted as sheep for the slaughter. Nay, in all these things we are more than conquerors, through him that hath loved us.

May not this make us ashamed of our cold, dead hearts that we hear so often of Christ, and—of his glorious excellencies and his wonderful love, with so little emotion—our hearts being very commonly frozen up like a clod of earth by worldly affections. And it may be that now and then with much difficulty we persuade ourselves to do a little or expend a little for the advancement of Christ's kingdom. And then are ready to boast of it, that we have done so nobly. Such superior examples as we have are enough to make us forever blush for our own attainments in the love of Christ, and rouse us earnestly to follow after those who have gone so far beyond us.

Third, the apostle lived in a day when Christianity was greatly despised. Yet he was not ashamed of the gospel of Christ. Christians were everywhere despised by the great men of the world. Almost all those that made any figure in the world, men in honorable stations, men of learning, and men of wealth, despised Christianity, and accounted it a mean, contemptible thing to be a Christian, a follower and worshiper of a poor, crucified man. To be a Christian was regarded as what ruined a man's reputation. Christians were everywhere looked upon as fools, and were derided and mocked. They were the meanest of mankind, the offscouring of the world. This was a great temptation to Christians to be ashamed of the gospel.

And the apostle Paul was more especially in such circumstances, as exposed him to this temptation. For, before he was a Christian, he was in great reputation among his own countrymen. He was esteemed a young man of more than ordinary proficiency in learning, and was a man of high distinction among the Pharisees, a class of men of the first standing among the Jews.

In times when religion is much despised, great men are more ready to be ashamed of it than others. Many of the great seem to think that to appear religious men would make them look little. They do not know how to comply with showing a devout spirit, a spirit of supreme love to God, and a strict regard to God's commands. But yet the apostle was not ashamed of the gospel of Christ anywhere, or before any person. He was not ashamed of it among his own countrymen, the Jews, before their rulers, and scribes, and great men, but ever boldly professed it, and confronted them in their opposition. When he was at Athens, the chief seat of learning and of learned men in the world, though the learned men and philosophers there despised his doctrine, and called him a babbler for preaching the gospel. Yet he felt no shame, but boldly disputed with and confounded those great philosophers, and converted some of them. And when he came to Rome, the metropolis and mistress of the world, where resided the emperor, and senators, and the chief rulers of the world, he was not ashamed of the gospel there. He tells the Romans;

> I am ready to preach the gospel to you that are at Rome also. For I am not ashamed of the gospel of Christ; for it is the power of God unto salvation to every one that believeth.

The apostle was greatly derided and despised for preaching a crucified Jesus. 1 Cor. 4:13, "We are made as the filth of the world, and are the offscouring of all things unto this day." And in the tenth verse he says, "We are fools for Christ's sake." They were everywhere accounted and called fools. Yet the apostle was so far from being ashamed of the crucified Jesus, that he gloried in him above all things. Gal. 6:14, "God forbid that I should glory, save in the cross of our Lord Jesus Christ."

Here is an example for us to follow, if at any time we fall in among those who hold religion in contempt, and will despise us for our pretensions to religion, and will be ready to deride us for being so precise, and look upon us as fools; that we may not be ashamed of religion, and yield to sinful compliances with vain and loose persons, lest we should appear singular, and be looked upon as ridiculous. Such a meanness of spirit possesses many persons who are not worthy to be called Christians; and are such as Christ will be ashamed of when he comes in the glory of his Father with the holy angels.

Fourth, another virtue in which we ought to follow the apostle was his contempt of the world, and his heavenly-mindedness. He contemned [held in contempt] all the vain enjoyments of the world. He despised its riches. Acts. 20:33, "I have coveted no man's silver, or gold, or apparel." He despised the pleasures of the world. "I keep under my body." The apostle's pleasures were in the sufferings of his body, instead of the gratification of its carnal appetites. 2 Cor. 12:10, "Therefore I take pleasure in infirmities, in reproaches, in necessities, in persecutions, in distresses, for Christ's sake." He despised the honors of the world. 1 Thes. 2:6, "Nor of men sought we glory; neither of you, nor yet of others." He declares that the world was crucified unto him, and he unto the world. These were not the things that the apostle sought, but the things that were above, that were out of sight to other men. 2 Cor. 4:18, "While we look not at the things which are seen, but at the things which are not seen." He longed greatly after heaven. 2 Cor. 5:4:

> For we that are in this tabernacle do groan, being burdened; not for that we would be unclothed, but clothed upon, that mortality might be swallowed up in life.

And he tells us that he knew no man after the flesh. That is, he did not look upon the men or things of this world, or regard them as related to the world, or as they respected the present life. But he considered all men and all things as they had relation to a spiritual nature, and to another world. In this the apostle acted as becomes a Christian. For Christians, those that are indeed so, are people that belong not to this world, and therefore, it is very unbecoming in them to have their minds taken up about these things. The example of Paul may make all such persons ashamed, who have their minds chiefly occupied about the things of the world, about gaining estates, or acquiring honors. And yet would be accounted fellow-disciples with the apostle, partakers of the same labors, and fellow-heirs of the same heavenly inheritance. And it should prompt us to strive for more indifference to the world, and for more heavenly-mindedness.

Fifth, we ought also to follow the example of the apostle in his abounding in prayer and praise. He was very earnest, and greatly engaged in those duties, and continued in them, as appears from many passages.

First, I thank my God through Jesus Christ for you all, that your faith is spoken of throughout the whole world. For God is my witness, whom I serve with my spirit in the gospel of his Son, that without ceasing I make mention of you always in my prayers. (Rom. 1:8.)

Wherefore I also, after I heard of your faith in the Lord Jesus and love unto all the saints, cease not to give thanks for you, making mention of you in my prayers. (Eph. 1:15, 16.)

We give thanks to God, and the Father of our Lord Jesus Christ, praying always for you. (Col. 1:3.)

We give thanks to God always for you all, making mention of you in our prayers; remembering without ceasing your work of faith and labor of love, and patience of hope in our Lord Jesus Christ, in the sight of God and our Father. (1 Thes. 1:2, 3.)

For what thanks can we render to God again for you, for all the joy wherewith we joy for your sakes before our God; night and day praying exceedingly, that we might see your face, and might perfect that which is lacking in your faith? (1 Thes. 3:9, 10.)

I thank God, whom I serve from my forefathers with pure conscience, that without ceasing I have remembrance of thee in my prayers, night and day. (2 Tim. 1:3.)

Sixth, we ought to follow him in his contentment under the allotments of Divine Providence. He was the subject of a vast variety of dispensations of Providence. He went through a great many changes, and was almost continually in suffering circumstances, sometimes in one respect, sometimes in another, and sometimes the subject of a great many kinds of suffering together. But yet he had attained to such a degree of submission to the will of God, as to be contented in every condition, and under all dispensations towards him. Phil. 4:11–13:

> Not that I speak in respect of want, for I have learned in whatsoever state I am, therewith to be content. I know both how to be abased, and I know how to abound. Every where, and in all things, I am instructed both to be full and to be hungry, both to abound and to suffer need. I can do all things through Christ which strengtheneth me.

What a blessed temper and disposition of mind was this to which Paul had arrived. And how happy is that man of whom it can now be said with truth! He is, as it were, out the reach of every evil. Nothing can touch him so as to disturb his rest, for he rests in everything that God orders.

Seventh, we should follow the apostle in his great caution in giving an account of his experience, not to represent more of himself in his words, than men should see in his deeds. In 2 Corinthians he gives somewhat of an account how he had been favored with visions and revelations, and had been caught up to the third heavens. And in the sixth verse (2 Cor. 12:6), intimating that he could relate more, he breaks off, and forbears to say anything further respecting his experience. And he gives this reason for it; *viz.* that he would avoid, in what he relates of himself, giving occasion for anyone to be disappointed in him, in expecting more from him, by his own account of his experience and revelations, than he should see or hear of him in his conversation. His words are:

> for though I would desire to glory, I shall not be a fool; for I will say the truth; but now I forbear, lest any man should think of me above that which he seeth me to be; or that he heareth of me.

Some may wonder at this in such a man as the apostle, and may say, "Why should a man so eminent in his conversation, be so cautious in this matter? Why need he be afraid to declare all the extraordinary things that he had witnessed, since his life was so agreeable, so eminently answerable to his experience?" But yet you see the apostle forbore upon this very account. He knew there was great need of caution in this matter. He knew that if in giving an account of his extraordinary revelations, he should give rise to an expectation of too great things in his conversation, and should not live answerably to that expectation, it would greatly wound religion. He knew that its enemies would be ready to say presently, "Who is this? The man that gives so extraordinary an account of his visions and revelations, and peculiar tokens of God's favor to him, does he live no more conformably to it?"

But if such a man as the apostle, so eminent in his life, was so cautious in this respect; surely we have need to be cautious, who fail so much more in our example than he did, and in whose conversation the enemy may find so much more occasion to speak reproachfully of religion. This teaches us that it would be better to refrain wholly from boasting of our experience than to represent ourselves as better than our deeds and conversation represent us. For men will compare one with the other. And if they do not see a correspondence between them, this will be much more to the dishonor of God than our account will be to his honor. Let Christians, therefore, be warned to be ever cautious in this respect, after the great example of the apostle.

3. I shall mention some of those virtues of the apostle that more immediately respected men, in which we ought to follow his example.

First, his meekness under abuses and his love to his enemies. There were multitudes that hated him, but there is no appearance of his hating any. The greater part of the world where he went were his enemies. But he was the friend of everyone and labored and prayed earnestly for the good of all. And when he was reproached and derided and buffeted, still it was with meekness and gentleness of spirit that he bore all, and wished well to them none the less, and sought their good. 1 Cor. 4:12, 13, "Being reviled, we bless; being persecuted, we suffer it; being defamed, we entreat."

In that period of his great sufferings when he went up to Jerusalem, and there was such an uproar about him, and the people were in so furious a rage against him, eagerly thirsting for his blood; he discovered no anger or ill will towards his persecutors. At that time when he was a prisoner through their malice, and stood before king Agrippa, and Agrippa said, "Almost thou persuadest me to be a Christian;" and his blood-thirsty enemies were standing by; he replied, "I would to God, that not only thou, but also all that hear me this day, were both almost and altogether such as I am, except these bonds." He wished that his accusers, and those who had bound themselves with an oath that they would neither eat nor drink till they had killed him, had all of them as great privileges and as much of the favor of heaven as himself. And that they were altogether as he was, except his bonds and imprisonment, and those afflictions which they had brought upon him. He did not desire that they should be like him in that affliction, though it was the fruit of their own cruelty.

And when some of the Corinthians, whom he had instructed and converted from heathenism, had dealt ill by him, had hearkened to some false teachers, that had been among them, who hated and reproached the apostle, he tells them, in 2 Cor. 12:15, notwithstanding these abuses, that still he would very gladly spend and be spent for them, though the more abundantly he loved them, the less he should be loved by them. If they returned him no thanks for his love, but only ill will and ill treatment, still he stood ready to spend and be spent for them.

And though the apostle was so hated, and had suffered so many abuses from the unbelieving Jews, yet how does he express his love to them? He prayed earnestly for them. Rom. 10:1: "Brethren, my heart's desire and prayer to God for Israel is that they might be saved." And he went mourning for them. He went about with a heavy heart, and with continual grief and sorrow, from compassion for them, under the calamities of which they were the subjects. And he declares in the most solemn manner, that he had so great desire for their salvation, that he could find it in his heart to wish himself accursed from Christ for them, and to be offered up a sacrifice, if that might be a means of their salvation. (Rom. 9:1–3.) We are to understand it of a temporal curse. He could be willing to die an accursed death, and so be made a curse for a time, as Christ was, if that might be a means of salvation to them.

How are those reproved by this, who, when they are abused and suffer reproach or injury, have thereby indulged a spirit of hatred against their neighbor, a prejudice whereby they are always apt to entertain a distrust, and to seek and embrace opportunities against them, and to be sorry for their prosperity, and glad at their disappointments.

Secondly, he delighted in peace. When any contention happened among Christians, he was exceedingly grieved by it, as when he heard of the contentions that broke out in the Corinthian church. He intimates to the Philippians, how he should rejoice at their living in love and peace, and therefore earnestly entreats them that they should so live. Phil. 2:1, 2:

> If there be therefore any consolation in Christ, if any comfort of love, if any fellowship of the Spirit, if any bowels and mercies, fulfil ye my joy, that ye be like-minded, having the same love, being of one accord, of one mind.

And he studied those things that should make for peace. To that end he yielded to everyone as much as possible in those things that were lawful, and complied with the weakness and humors of others oftentimes, for the sake of peace. He declares that though he was free from all men, yet he had made himself servant of all. To the Jews he became as a Jew; to

them that were under the law, as under the law; to them that were without law, as without law; to the weak he became as weak. He rather chose
to please others than himself, for the sake of peace, and the good of their
souls. 1 Cor. 10:33, "Even as I please all men in all things, not seeking
mine own profit, but the profit of many, that they may be saved."

*Third, he was of a most tender compassionate spirit towards any that were
in affliction.* He showed such a spirit especially in the case of the incestuous Corinthian. The crime was very great, and the fault of the church was
great in suffering such wickedness among them, and this occasioned the
apostle to write with some sharpness to them respecting it.

But when the apostle perceived that his reproof was laid to heart by
the Corinthian Christians, and that they repented and their hearts were
filled with sorrow, though he rejoiced at it, yet he was so affected with
their sorrow, that his heart yearned towards them, and he was almost
ready to repent that he had written so severely to them. He was full of
concern about it, lest his former letter should have filled them with over-
much sorrow.

> For though I made you sorry with a letter, I do not repent, though I did re-
> pent; for I perceive that the same epistle hath made you sorry, though it
> were but for a season.

So he had compassion for the incestuous man, though he had been guilty
of so vile a crime, and was greatly concerned that he should be comforted. Whenever any Christian suffered or was hurt, the apostle says he
felt it and suffered himself. 2 Cor. 11:29, "Who is weak, and I am not
weak? Who is offended, and I burn not?"

Fourth, he rejoiced at others' prosperity and joy. When he saw the soul of
anyone comforted, the apostle was a sharer with him. His soul was comforted also. When he saw any Christian refreshed in his spirit, his own
spirit was refreshed. 2 Cor. 7:6, 7:

> Nevertheless, God that comforteth those that are cast down, comforted us
> by the coming of Titus; and not by his coming only, but by the consolation
> wherewith he was comforted in you, when he told us your earnest desire,
> your mourning, your fervent mind toward me, so that I rejoiced the more.

> Therefore we were comforted in your comfort; yea, and exceedingly the
> more joyed we for the joy of Titus, because his spirit was refreshed by you all.

Fifth, he delighted in the fellowship of God's people. He longed after them
when absent. Phil. 1:8, "For God is my record how greatly I long after

you in the bowels of Christ." And also, "Therefore, my brethren, dearly beloved and longed for, my joy and crown." So Rom. 1:11, 12:

> For I long to see you, that I may impart unto you some spiritual gift, to the end ye may be established; that is, that I may be comforted together with you by the mutual faith both of you and me.

Sixth, he was truly courteous in his behavior towards others. Though he was so great a man, and had so much honor put upon him of God, yet he was full of courtesy towards all men, rendering to all suitable respect. Thus when he was called before Jewish or heathen magistrates, he treated them with the honor and respect due to their places. When the Jews took him in the temple, though they behaved themselves more like devils than men, yet he addressed them in terms of high respect, "Men, brethren, and fathers, hear ye my defense:" calling the common Jews his *brethren*, and saluting the elders and scribes with the title of *fathers*, though they were a body of infidels. So when he pleads his cause before Festus, a heathen governor, he gives him the title that belonged to him in his station; calling him, "Most noble Festus." His courtesy also appears in his salutations in his epistles. He is particularly careful to mention many persons, directing that his salutations should be given to them. Such a degree of courtesy, in so great a person as this apostle, reproves all those professing Christians, who, though far below him, are not courteous and respectful in their behavior to their neighbors, and especially to their superiors. Incivility is here reproved, and the too common neglect of Christians is reproved, who do not take strict care, that their children are taught good manners, and politeness, and brought up in a respectful and courteous behavior towards others.

4. I shall mention those virtues of the apostle that respected both God and men, in which we should imitate his example.

First, he was a man of a most public spirit. He was greatly concerned for the prosperity of Christ's kingdom, and the good of his church. We see a great many men wholly engaged in pursuit of their worldly interests. Many who are earnest in the pursuit of the carnal pleasures, many who are eager in the pursuit of honors, and many who are violent in the pursuit of gain. But we probably never saw any man more engaged to advance his estate, nor more taken up with his pleasures, nor more greedy of honor, than the apostle Paul was about the flourishing of Christ's kingdom, and the good of the souls of men.

The things that grieve other men are outward crosses: losses in estates, or falling under contempt, or bodily sufferings. But these things grieved not him. He made little account of them. The things that grieved him were those that hurt the interests of religion. And about those his tears were shed. Thus he was exceedingly grieved, and wept greatly, for the corruptions that had crept into the church of Corinth, which was the occasion of his writing his first epistle to them. 2 Cor. 2:4, "For out of much affliction and anguish of heart, I wrote unto you, with many tears."

The things about which other men are jealous, are their worldly advantages and pleasures. If these are threatened, their jealously is excited, since they are above all things, dear to them. But the things that kindled the apostle's jealousy, were those that seemed to threaten the interests of religion, and the good of the church: 2 Cor. 11:2, 3:

> For I am jealous over you with a godly jealousy; for I have espoused you to one husband, that I may present you as a chaste virgin to Christ. But I fear, lest by any means, as the serpent beguiled Eve through his subtlety, so your minds should be corrupted from the simplicity that is in Christ.

The things at which other men rejoice are their amassing earthly treasures, their being advanced to honors, their being possessed of outward pleasures and delights. But these excited not the apostle's joy; but when he saw or heard of anything by which the interests of religion were promoted, and the church of Christ prospered, then he rejoiced: 1 Thes. 1:3, "Remembering without ceasing your work of faith and labor of love, and patience of hope in our Lord Jesus Christ, in the sight of God and our Father." And chapter 2:20, "Ye are our glory and joy." He rejoiced at those things, however dear they cost him, how much soever he lost by them in his temporal interest, if the welfare of religion and the good of souls were promoted. Phil. 2:16, 17:

> Holding forth the word of life, that I may rejoice in the day of Christ, that I have not run in vain, neither labored in vain. Yea, and if I be offered upon the sacrifice and service of your faith, I joy and rejoice with you all.

He rejoiced at the steadfastness of saints: Col. 2:5, "For though I be absent in the flesh, yet am I with you in the spirit, joying and beholding your order, and the steadfastness of your faith in Christ." And he rejoiced at the conviction of sinners, and in whatever tended to it.

He rejoiced at any good which was done, though by others, and though it was done accidentally by his enemies. Phil. 1:15–18:

> Some indeed preach Christ even of envy and strife; and some also of good will. The one preach Christ of contention, not sincerely, supposing to add

affliction to my bonds. But the other of love, knowing that I am set for the defense of the gospel. What then? Notwithstanding, every way, whether in pretense or in truth, Christ is preached; and I therein do rejoice, yea, and will rejoice.

When the apostle heard anything of this nature, it was good news to him: 1 Thes. 3:6, 7:

> But now, when Timotheus came from you unto us, and brought us good tidings of your faith and charity, and that ye have good remembrance of us always, desiring greatly to see us, as we also you; therefore, brethren, we were comforted over you in all our affliction and distress by your faith.

When he heard such tidings, his heart was wont to be enlarged in the praises of God: Col. 1:3, 4:

> We give thanks to God and the Father or our Lord Jesus Christ, praying always for you, since we heard of your faith in Christ Jesus, and of the love which ye have to all the saints.

He was not only wont to praise God when he first heard such tidings, but as often as he thought of such things, they were so joyful to him, that he readily praised God. Phil. 1:3–5:

> I thank my God upon every remembrance of you, always in every prayer of mine for you all making request with joy, for your fellowship in the gospel from the first day until now.

Let us compare ourselves with such an example, and examine how far we are of such spirit. Let those on this occasion reflect upon themselves, whose hearts are chiefly engaged in their own private temporal concerns, and are not much concerned respecting the interests of religion and the church of Christ, if they can obtain their private aims; who are greatly grieved when things go contrary to their worldly prosperity, who see religion, as it were, weltering in its blood, without much sorrow of heart. It may be, that they will say; "It is greatly to be lamented that there is such declension, and it is a sorrowful thing that sin so much prevails." But if we would look into their hearts, how cold and careless should we see them. Those words are words, of course. They express themselves thus chiefly, because they think it creditable to lament the decay of religion. But they are ten times as much concerned about other things as these, about their own private interest, or some secular affairs of the town. If anything seems to threaten their being disappointed in these things, how readily are they excited and alarmed. But how quiet and easy in their spirit, notwithstanding all the dark clouds that appear over the cause and kingdom of Christ, and the salvation of those around them! How quick and how high is their zeal against those, who, they think, unjustly oppose them in their temporal interests. But how low is their zeal, comparatively, against those things that are exceedingly pernicious of the interests of religion! If their own credit is touched, how are they awakened! But they can see the credit of religion wounded, and bleeding, and dying, with little hearty concern. Most men are of a private, narrow spirit. They are not of the spirit of the apostle Paul, nor of the psalmist, who preferred Jerusalem before his chief joy. (Psa. 137:6.)

Secondly, we ought to follow the apostle in his diligent and laborious endeavors to do good. We see multitudes incessantly laboring and striving after the world. But not more than the apostle labored to advance the kingdom of his dear Master and the good of his fellow-creatures. His work was very great, and attended with great difficulties and opposition. And his labor was answerably great. He labored abundantly more than any of the apostles: 1 Cor. 15:10, "I labored more abundantly than they all, yet not I, but the grace of God which was with me."

How great were the pains he took in preaching and in traveling from place to place over so great part of the world, by sea and land, and probably for the most part on foot, when he traveled by land: instructing and converting the heathen, disputing with gainsayers, and heathen Jews, and heretics, strenuously opposing and fighting against the enemies of the church of Christ, wrestling not with flesh and blood, but against principalities and powers, against the rulers of the darkness of this world, against spiritual wickedness in high places; acting the part of a good soldier, as one that goes to warfare, putting on Christ and using the whole armor of God, laboring to establish and confirm and build up the saints, reclaiming those that were wandering, delivering those that were ensnared, enlightening the dark, comforting the disconsolate, and succoring the tempted, rectifying disorders that had happened in churches, exercising ecclesiastical discipline towards offenders, and admonishing the saints of the covenant of grace, opening and applying the Scriptures, ordaining persons and giving them directions, and assisting those that were ordained, and writing epistles, and sending messengers to one and another part of the church of Christ!

He had the care of the churches lying continually upon him. 2 Cor. 11:28, "Besides those things that are without, that which cometh upon me daily, the care of all the churches." These things occasioned him to be continually engaged in earnest labor. He continued in it night and day, sometimes almost the whole night, preaching and admonishing, as appears by Acts 20:7,11:

> And upon the first day of the week, when the disciples came together to break bread, Paul preached unto them, ready to depart on the morrow, and continued his speech until midnight. When he therefore was come up again, and had broken bread, and eaten, and talked a long while, even till break of day, so he departed.

And he did all freely, without any view to any temporal gain. He tells the Corinthians that he would gladly spend and be spent for them. Besides his laboring in the work of the gospel, he labored very much, yea, sometimes night and day, in a handicraft trade to procure subsistence, that he might not be chargeable to others, and so hinder the gospel of Christ: 1 Thes. 2:9,

> For ye remember, brethren, our labor and travail, for laboring night and day, because we would not be chargeable unto any of you, we preached unto you the gospel of God.

And he continued this course of labor as long as he lived. He never was weary in well-doing; and though he met with continual opposition, and thousands of difficulties, yet nothing discouraged him. But he kept on, pressing forward in this course of hard, constant labor to the end of his life, as appears by what he says just before his death, 2 Tim. 4:6, 7:

> I am now ready to be offered, and the time of my departure is at hand. I have fought a good fight, I have finished my course, I have kept the faith.

And the effects and fruits of the apostle's labors witnessed for him. The world was blessed by the good he did; not one nation only, but multitudes of nations. The effects of his labors were so great, in so many nations, before he had labored twenty years, that the heathens called it "his turning the world upside down." (Acts 27:6.) This very man was the chief instrument in that great work of God, the calling of the Gentiles, and the conversion of the Roman world. And he seems to have done more good, far more good, than any other man ever did from the beginning of the world to this day. He lived after his conversion not much more than thirty years. And in those thirty years he did more than a thousand men commonly do in an age.

This example may well make us reflect upon ourselves, and consider how little we do for Christ, and for our fellow-creatures. We profess to be Christians as well as the apostle Paul, and Christ is worthy that we should serve him as Paul did. But how small are our labors for God and Christ and our fellow creatures! Though many of us keep ourselves busy, how are our labor and strength spent, and with what is our time filled up? Let us consider ourselves a little, and the manner of spending our time. We labor to provide for ourselves and families, to maintain ourselves in credit, and to make our part good among men. But is that all for which we are sent into the world? Did he who made us and gave us our powers of mind and strength of body, and who gives us our time and our talents, give them to us chiefly to be spent in this manner; or in serving him?

Many years have rolled over the heads of some of us, and what have we lived for? What have we been doing all this time? How much is the world the better for us? Were we here only to eat and to drink, and to devour the good which the earth produces? Many of the blessings of Providence have been conferred upon us. And where is the good that we have done in return? If we had never been born, or if we had died in infancy, of how much good would the world have been deprived of?

Such reflections should be made with concern, by those who pretend to be Christians. For certainly God does not plant vines in his vineyard, except for the fruit which he expects they should bring forth. He does not hire laborers into his vineyard, but to do service. They who live only for themselves, live in vain, and shall at last be cut down as cumberers of the earth. Let the example of Paul make us more diligent to do good for the time to come. Men that do but little good are very ready to excuse themselves, and to say that God has not succeeded their endeavors. But is it any wonder that we have not succeeded, when we have been no more engaged? When God sees any person thoroughly and earnestly engaged, continuing in it, and really faithful, he is wont to succeed [grant success to] them in some good measure. You see how wonderfully he succeeded the great labors of the apostle.

Third, he did not only encounter great labors, but he exercised also his utmost skill and contrivance for the glory of God, and the good of his fellow-creatures. 2 Cor. 12:16, "Being crafty, I caught you with guile." How do the men of the world not only willingly labor to obtain worldly good, but how much craft and subtlety do they use? And let us consider how it is here among ourselves. How many are our contrivances to secure and advance our own worldly concerns! Who can reckon up the number of all the schemes that have been formed among us, to gain money, and honors, and accomplish particular worldly designs? How subtle are we to avoid those things that might hurt us in our worldly interest, and to baffle the designs of those who may be endeavoring to hurt us! But how little is contrived for the advancement of religion, and the good of our neighbors! How many schemes are laid by men to promote their worldly designs, where [only] one is laid for the advancement of the kingdom of Christ, and the good of men! How frequent are the meetings of neighbors to determine how they may best advance such and such worldly affairs! But how seldom are there such meetings to revive sinking religion, to maintain and advance the credit of the gospel, and to accomplish charitable designs for the advancement of Christ's kingdom, and the comfort and well-being of mankind! May not these considerations justly be a source of lamentation? How many men are wise in promoting their worldly interests? But what a shame is it that so few show themselves wise as serpents and harmless as doves for Christ! And how commonly is it the reverse of what the apostle advises the Christian Romans, "I would have you wise unto that which is good, and simple concerning evil." Is it not often on the contrary with professing Christians, as it was with the people of Judah and Jerusalem? "They are wise to do evil, but to do good, they have no knowledge?"

Fourth, the apostle Paul did willingly forego those thing that were in themselves lawful, for the furtherance of the interests of religion and the good of men. Thus marriage was a thing lawful for the apostle Paul as well as for other men, as he himself asserts. But he did not use the liberty he had in this matter because he thought he might be under greater advantages to spread the gospel in a single than a married state. So it was lawful for the apostle to take the other course of life, as in eating and drinking, and freely using all kinds of wholesome food. And it was in itself a lawful thing for the apostle to demand a maintenance of those to whom he preached. But he forbore those things because he supposed that in his circumstances, and in the circumstances of the church of Christ in that day, he could more advance the interests of religion and the good of men without them.

For the gospel's sake, and for the good of men, he was willing to forego all the outward advantages he could derive from them. 1 Cor. 8:13, "Wherefore if meat make my brother to offend, I will eat no meat while the world standeth, lest I make my brother to offend." He would not only avoid those things that were useless in themselves, but those also that gave any occasion to sin, or which led or exposed either himself or others to sin. Then it follows in the next chapter:

Am I not an apostle? Am I not free? Have I not seen Jesus Christ our Lord? Are not ye my work in the Lord? If I be not an apostle unto others, yet doubtless I am to you; for the seal of mine apostleship are ye in the Lord. Mine answer to them that do examine me is this, "Have we not power to eat and to drink? Have we not power to lead about a sister, a wife, as well as other apostles, and as the brethren of the Lord, and Cephas? Or I only and Barnabas, have not we power to forbear working?"

The apostle did not only forbear some little things, but he put himself to great difficulties by forbearing those thing that were in themselves lawful. It cost him a great deal of labor of body to maintain himself. But yet he willingly labored, working with his own hands. And as he says, though he was free from all men, yet he made himself the servant of all, that he might gain the more.

Let this induce such persons to consider themselves, whether they act altogether as become Christians, who look upon it as a sufficient excuse for all the liberties they take, that the things in which they allow themselves, are in themselves lawful, that they are nowhere forbidden, though they cannot deny but that considered in their circumstances, they are not of ill tendency, and expose them to temptation, and really tend to wound the credit and interest of religion, and to be a stumbling-block to others, or, as the apostle expresses it, tend to cause others to offend. But they uphold themselves with this, that the things which they practice are not absolutely unlawful in themselves, and therefore they will not hearken to any counsels to avoid them. They think with themselves that it is unreasonable they should be tied up so strictly, that they may not take one and another liberty, and must be so stiff and precise above others.

But why did not the apostle talk after their manner? Why did not he say within himself, "It is unreasonable that I should deny myself lawful meat and drink merely to comply with the consciences of a few weak persons, that are unreasonable in their scruples? Why should I deny myself the comforts of marriage? Why should I deny myself that maintenance which Christ himself has ordained for ministers, only to avoid the objection of unreasonable men?" But the apostle was of another spirit. What he aimed at was by any means to promote the interest of religion and the good of the church. And he had rather forego all the common comforts and enjoyments of life than that religion should suffer.

Fifth, the apostle willingly endured innumerable and extreme sufferings for the honor of Christ and the good of men. His sufferings were very great; and that not only once or twice, but he went through a long series of sufferings, that continued from the time of his conversion as long as his life lasted. So that his life was not only a life of extraordinary labor, but a life of extreme sufferings also. Labors and sufferings were mixed together, and attended each other to the end of the race which he ran. He endured sufferings of all kinds, even those that cannot consist in the loss of temporal things. He tells us that he had suffered the loss of all things, Phil. 3:8, all his former enjoyments, which he had before his conversion. And he endured many kinds of positive afflictions. In 1 Cor. 4:11, 12:

> Even unto this present hour, we both hunger and thirst, and are naked, and are buffeted, and have no certain dwelling-place; and labor, working with our hands: being reviled, we bless; being persecuted, we suffer it.

From 2 Cor. 6:4–11:

> But in all things approving ourselves as the ministers of God, in much patience, in afflictions, in necessities, in distresses, in stripes, in imprisonments, in tumults, in labors, in watchings, in fastings; by pureness, by knowledge, by long-suffering, by kindness, by the Holy Ghost, by love unfeigned, by the word of truth, by the power of God, by the armor of righteousness on the right hand and on the left, by honor and dishonor, by evil report and good report: as deceivers, and yet true; as unknown, and yet well known; as dying, and behold we live; as chastened, and not killed; as sorrowful, yet always rejoicing; as poor, yet making many rich; as having nothing, and yet possessing all things.

None of the apostles went through so great and such various afflictions as he. See 2 Cor. 11:23–28:

> Are they ministers of Christ? I am more; in labors more abundant, in stripes above measure, in prisons more frequent, in deaths oft. Of the Jews five times received I forty stripes save one. Thrice was I beaten with rods, once was I stoned, thrice I suffered shipwreck, a night and a day I have been in the deep; in journeyings often, in perils of waters, in perils of robbers, in perils by mine own countrymen, in perils by the heathen, in perils in the city, in perils in the wilderness, in perils in the sea, in perils among false brethren; in weariness and painfulness, in watchings often, in hunger and thirst, in fastings often, in cold and nakedness.

His sufferings were so extreme that he did not go through a series of sufferings merely, but might be said, as it were, to go through a series of deaths. He did in effect endure the pains of death over and over again almost continually, and therefore he expresses himself as he does. In 2 Cor. 4:9–11:

> Persecuted, but not forsaken; cast down, but not destroyed; always bearing about in the body the dying of the Lord Jesus, that the life also of Jesus might

be made manifest in our body. For we which live are always delivered unto death for Jesus' sake, that the life also of Jesus might be made manifest in our mortal flesh.

From Rom. 8:36, "As it is written, For thy sake we are killed all the day long; we are accounted as sheep for the slaughter." 1 Cor. 15:31, "I protest by your rejoicing, which I have in Christ Jesus our Lord, I die daily." He was so pursued and pressed by troubles, sometimes outward and inward troubles together, that he had no rest. 2 Cor. 7:5, "For when we were come into Macedonia, our flesh had no rest, but we were troubled on every side: without were fightings, within were fears." Sometimes his sufferings were so extreme that his nature seemed just ready to faint under them: 2 Cor. 1:8, "for we would not, brethren, have you ignorant of our trouble, which came to us in Asia, that we were pressed out of measure above strength, insomuch that we despaired even of life." And at last the apostle was deprived of his life. He suffered a violent death at Rome under the hand of that cruel tyrant, Nero, soon after he wrote the second epistle of Timothy.

These things he endured for Christ's sake, for the advancement of his kingdom, as he says, he was always delivered to death for Jesus' sake. And those he endured also from love to men, and from an earnest desire of their good. 2 Tim. 2:10, "Therefore I endure all things for the elect's sake, that they may also obtain the salvation which is in Christ Jesus with eternal glory." He knew that afflictions awaited him beforehand. But he would not avoid his duty because of such afflictions. He was so resolute in seeking Christ's glory, and the good of men, that he would pursue these objects, notwithstanding what might befall him. Acts 20:22–24:

> And now, behold, I go bound in the spirit unto Jerusalem, not knowing the things that shall befall me there; save that the Holy Ghost witnesseth in every city, saying that bonds and afflictions abide me. But none of these things move me, neither count I my life dear unto myself, so that I might finish my course with joy, and the ministry, which I have received of the Lord Jesus, to testify the gospel of the grace of God.

Yet he went through them cheerfully and willingly, and delighted to do God's will, and to promote others' good, though it was at this great cost. Col. 1:24, "Who now rejoice in my sufferings for you, and fill up that which is behind of the afflictions of Christ in my flesh for his body's sake, which is the church." And he was never weary. He did not, after he had suffered a long time, excuse himself, and say he thought he had done his part.

Now here appears Christianity in its proper colors. To be of such a spirit as this, is to be of such a spirit as Christ so often requires of us, if we would be his disciples. This is to sell all and give to the poor. This is to take up the cross daily and follow Christ. To have such a spirit as this, is to have good evidence of being a Christian indeed, a thorough Christian, one that has given himself to Christ without reserve, one that hates father and mother, and wife, and children, and sisters, yea and his own life also, one that loses his life for Christ's sake, and so shall find it.

And though it is not required of all that they should endure so great sufferings as Paul did, yet it is required and absolutely necessary, that many Christians should be in a measure of this spirit, should be of a spirit to lose all things and suffer all things for Christ, rather than not obey his commands and seek his glory. How well may our having such an example as this set before our eyes make us ashamed, who are so backward now and then to lose little things, to put ourselves a little out of our way, to deny ourselves some convenience, to deny our sinful appetites, or to incur the displeasure of a neighbor. Alas! what thought have we of Christianity, to make much of such things as these, to make so many objections, to keep back, and contrive ways to excuse ourselves, when a little difficulty arises! What kind of thoughts had we of being Christians, when we first undertook to be such, or first pretended a willingness to be Christians? Did we never sit down and count the cost, or did we cast it up at this rate, that we thought the whole sum would not amount to such little sufferings as lie in our way?

II. I now proceed to show under what special obligations we are to follow the good example of this apostle.

Beside the obligation that rests upon us to follow the good example of all, and beside the eminence of his example, there are some special reasons why we are under greater obligations to be influenced by the good example of this great apostle than by the very same example in others. This appears if we consider,

1. In general, that those whom God has especially appointed to be teachers in the Christian church, he has also set to be examples in his church. It is part of the charge that belongs to teachers, to be examples to others. It is one thing that belongs to their work and office. So this is part of the charge that the apostle gives to Timothy, "Be thou an example of the believers, in word, in conversation, in charity, in spirit, in faith, in purity." The same charge is given to Titus, "In all things showing thyself a pattern of good works." And this is part of the charge the apostle Peter gives to the elders and teachers of the Christian church. "The elders which are among you, I exhort; feed the flock of God. Neither being lords over God's heritage, but being examples to the flock." Thus Christ, the chief Shepherd of the sheep, whom God ordained to be the greatest teacher, he also ordained to be the greatest example to his church. And so those shepherds and teachers that are under him, according as they are appointed to be teachers, are also to be examples. They are to be guides of the flock in two ways, viz. by teaching and by example, as shepherds lead their flocks in two ways: partly by their voice by calling them, and partly by going before them, and by leading the way. And indeed guiding by word and guiding by example, are but two different ways of teaching; and therefore both alike belong to the office of teachers in the Christian church.

But if this be so, if God has especially set those to be examples in the Christian church whom he has made its teachers, then it will follow, that wherever they have left us good examples, those examples are especially to be regarded. For God has doubtless made the duty of teachers towards the church, and the duty of the church towards her teachers, to answer one another. And therefore the charge is mutual. The charge is not only to teachers to set good examples, but the charge is to the church to regard and follow their good examples. Heb. 13:7, "Remember them which have the rule over you, which have spoken unto you the Word of God, whose faith follow, considering the end of their conversation." It is with respect to the good examples of the teachers of the Christian church, as it is with their words, their instructions and exhortations. We ought to hear good instructions and good counsels of anyone, let him be whom he may. But yet we are under special obligations to hearken to the good instructions and examples of those whom God has made our teachers. For that is the very office to which God has appointed them to teach and to counsel us.

2. There are two things that are to be observed in particular of the apostle Paul which, from the foregoing general observation, will show that we are under very special obligations to regard and follow his good example.

First, God has appointed the apostle Paul not only to be a greater teacher of the Christian church in that age in which he lived, but the principal teacher of his church of any mere man in all succeeding ages. He was set of God not only to teach the church then, when he lived, but God has made him our teacher by his inspired writings. The Christian church is taught by the apostle still, and has been in every age since he lived. It is not with the penmen of the Scriptures, as it is with other teachers of the Christian church. Other teachers are made the teachers of a particular flock in the age in which they live. But the penmen of the Scriptures has God made to be the teachers of the church universal in all ages. And therefore, as particular congregations ought to follow the good examples of their pastors, so the church universal in all ages ought to observe and follow the good examples of the prophets and apostles, that are the penmen of the Scriptures, in all ages.

So the apostle James commands us to take the ancient prophets for our example, because they have been appointed of God to be our teachers, and have spoken to us in the name of the Lord. Jam. 5:10, "Take, my brethren, the prophets, who have spoken in the name of the Lord, for an example of suffering affliction and patience." The prophets and apostles, in that God has made them penmen of the Scriptures, are, next to Christ, the foundation of the church of God. Eph. 2:20, "Built on the foundation of the prophets and apostles, Jesus Christ himself being the chief corner-stone." And Paul, above all the penmen of the Scriptures, is distinguished of God as being made by him the principal teacher of the Christian church of any mere man. Moses taught gospel truths under types and shadows, whereby he did, as it were, put a veil over his face. But Paul used great plainness of speech. (2 Cor. 3:12, 13.) Moses was a minister of the Old Testament and of the letter that kills. But the apostle Paul is the principal minister of the New Testament, of the spirit, and not of the letter. (2 Cor. 3:6, 7.) Christ has empowered this apostle to be the penmen of more of the New Testament than any other man, and it is by him chiefly that we have the great doctrines of it explained. And God has actually made this apostle the principal founder of the Christian church under Christ, which is a great obligation on the flock to regard and follow his good example.

Secondly, we who are Gentiles, are especially under obligations to regard his teaching and example because it has been mainly by means of this apostle that we have been brought into the Christian church. He was the great apostle of the Gentiles, the main instrument of that great work of God, the calling of the Gentiles. It was chiefly by his means that all the countries of Europe came by the gospel. And so it was through his hands that our nation came by the gospel. They either had the gospel from him immediately, or from those who had it from him. Had it not been for the labors of this apostle, our nation might have remained to this day in gross heathenism.

This consideration should especially engage us to regard him as our guide, and should endear his good example to us. The apostle often exhorts those churches, as the church of Corinth, Philippi, and others which he had converted from heathenism, and to which he had been a spiritual father: we are some of them. We have been the more remarkably converted from heathenism by this apostle, and we ought to acknowledge him as our spiritual father. And we are obliged to follow his good example as children should follow the good example of their parents.

General Application

Of the whole that has been said on this subject, which may be by way [summarized as:] of exhortation to all earnestly to endeavor to follow the good example of this great apostle.

We have heard what a spirit the apostle manifested, and after what manner he lived in the world, how earnestly he sought his own salvation, and that not only before, but also after his conversion, and how earnestly cautious he was to avoid eternal damnation, long after he had obtained a saving interest in Christ.

We have heard how strong he was in faith, how great was his love to his Lord and Savior, and how he was not ashamed of the gospel, but gloried in the cross of Christ, how he abounded in prayer and praise, how he contemned the wealth and pleasures and glory of the world, how contented he was with the allotments of Providence, how prudent and cautious he was in giving an account of his achievements, lest he should represent more of himself in words than men should see of him in deeds.

We have heard how much he suffered under abuses, how he loved his enemies, how he delighted in peace, and rejoiced with those that rejoiced, and wept with those that wept, and delighted in the fellowship of God's people, and how courteous he was in his behavior towards others.

We have heard of what a public spirit he was, how greatly concerned for the prosperity of Christ's kingdom and the good of his church, how diligent, laborious, and indefatigable in his endeavors to do good, how he studied for ways and means to promote this end, how he exercised his skill and contrivance, willingly foregoing those things that were in themselves lawful, and willingly enduring innumerable and extraordinary sufferings. My exhortation now is to imitate thus example; and to enforce this, I desire that several things may be considered.

I. Let it be considered, why it is that we have so much written of the good example of this apostle, unless that we might follow it.

We often read those things in the Holy Scriptures which have now been set before us on this subject; and to what purpose, unless we apply them to ourselves? We had as good never have been informed how well the apostle behaved himself, if we do not endeavor to follow him. We all profess to be Christians, and we ought to form our notions of Christianity from what is written in the Scriptures by the prophets, and from the precepts and excellent examples that are there set before us.

One great reason why many professors live no better, walk no more amiably, and are in so many things so unlovely is that they have not good notions of Christianity. They do not seem to have a right idea of that religion that is taught us in the New Testament. They have not well learned Christ. The notions that some persons entertain of Christianity are very distorted, and ill conformed to the gospel. The notions of others are very erroneous. They lay the chief stress wrong[ly] upon things on which it ought not to be laid. They place religion almost altogether in some particular duties, leaving out others of great weight, and, it may be, the weightier matters of the law.

And the reason why they have no better notions of Christianity is because they take their notions of it chiefly from those sources whence they ought not to take them. Some take them from the general cry or voice of the people, among whom they live. They see that others place religion merely, if not almost wholly, in such and such things. And hence their notions of Christianity are formed. Or they take their notions from the example of particular individuals now living, who are in great reputation for godliness. And their notion of Christianity is, that it consists in being like such persons. Hence they never have just notions of religion. 2 Cor. 10:12, "They, measuring themselves by themselves, and comparing themselves among themselves, are not wise."

If we would have right notions of Christianity, we should observe those in whom it shone, of whom we have an account in the Scriptures. For they are the examples that God himself has selected to set before us to that end, that from thence we might form our notions of religion, and especially the example of this apostle. God knows how to select examples. If therefore we would have right notions of Christianity, we ought to follow the good example of the apostle Paul. He was certainly a Christian indeed, and an eminent Christian. We have God's abundant testimony. But Christianity is in itself an amiable thing, and so it appeared in the example of this apostle. And if the professors of it would form their notions of it from such examples as those, rather than from any particular customs and examples that we have now, it would doubtless appear much more amiable in their practice than it now does. It would win others. They would not be a stumbling-block. Their light would shine. They would command reverence and esteem, and be of powerful influence.

II. If we follow the good example which this apostle has set us, it will secure to us the like comfortable and sweet influence of God, that he enjoyed through the course of his life.

Let us consider what a happy life the apostle lived, what peace of conscience, and joy in the Holy Ghost, he possessed. 2 Cor. 1:12, "for our rejoicing is this, the testimony of our conscience." How did he abound with comfort and joy, even in the midst of the greatest afflictions. 2 Cor. 1:3–5,

> Blessed by God, even the Father of our Lord Jesus Christ, the Father of mercies, and the God of all comfort. Who comforteth us in all our tribulation, that we may be able to comfort them which are in any trouble, by the comforts wherewith we ourselves are comforted of God. For was the sufferings of Christ abound in us, so our consolation also aboundeth in Christ.

In all his tribulation his joy was exceedingly great.

He seems to want words to express the greatness of the joy which he possessed continually. He says he was filled with comfort, and was exceedingly joyful. 2 Cor. 7:4, "I am filled with comfort, I am exceeding joyful in all our tribulation." How does the apostle's love seem to overflow with joy! 2 Cor. 6:10, 11:

> As sorrowful, yet always rejoicing; as poor, yet making many rich; as having nothing, yet possessing all things. O ye Corinthians, our mouth is open unto you, our heart is enlarged.

How happy is such a life! How well is such happiness worth pursuing! We are ourselves the occasion of our wounds and troubles. We bring darkness on our own souls. Professing Christians, by indulging their sloth, seek their own easy and comfort. But they defeat their own aim. The most laborious and the most self-denying Christians are the most happy. There are many who are complaining of their darkness, and inquiring what they shall do for light, and the comfortable presence of God.

III. This would be the way to be helped against temptation, and to triumph over our spiritual enemies as the apostle did.

Satan assaulted him violently, and men continually persecuted him. The powers of Hell combined against him. But God was with him, and made him more than a conqueror. He lived a life of triumph. 2 Cor. 2:14, "Now thanks be unto God, who always causeth us to triumph in Christ." Let us consider what an excellent privilege it would be thus to be helped against temptation. What a grief of mind is it to be so often overcome.

IV. This would secure us honor from God, and an extraordinary intimacy with him.

Moses enjoyed a great intimacy with God, but the apostle Paul in some respects a greater. Moses conversed with God in Mount Sinai. Paul was caught up to the third heavens. He had abundant visions and revelations more than he has told us, lest any should think him to boast. He was favored with more of the miraculous gifts of the Holy Spirit than any other person. And though we cannot expect to be honored with intimacy with heaven in just the same way, yet if we in good earnest apply ourselves, we may have greater and greater intimacy, so that we may come with boldness, and converse with God as a friend.

This would be the way to make us great blessings in the world. The apostle, by means of such a spirit and such a behavior as you have heard, was made the greatest blessing to the world of any who ever lived on earth, except the man Christ Jesus himself. Wherever he went, there went a blessing with him. To have him enter a city was commonly made a greater mercy to it than if the greatest monarch on earth had come there, scattering his treasures around him among the inhabitants. Wherever he went, there did, as it were, a light shine about him, seemingly to enlighten the benighted children of men. Silver and gold he had none. But what he imparted to many thousands was worth more to them than if he had bestowed upon them the richest jewels of which the Roman emperor was possessed.

And he was not only a blessing to that generation, but has been so since his death, by the fruits of what he did in his lifetime, the foundations he then laid, and by the writings which he has left for the good of mankind, to the end of the world. He then was, and ever since has been, a light to the church next in brightness to the Sun of righteousness. And it was by means of his excellent spirit and excellent behavior that he became such a blessing.

Those were the things that God made useful in him for doing so much good. And if we should imitate the apostle in such a spirit and behavior, the undoubted consequence would be that we also should be made great blessings in the world. We should not live in vain, but should carry a blessing with us wherever we went. Instead of being cumberers of the ground, multitudes would be fed with our fruit, and would have reason to praise and bless God that he ever gave us a being. Now, how melancholy a consideration may it be to any persons that they have lived to no purpose, that the world would have been deprived of nothing, if they had never been born, and it may be, have been better without them than with them! How desirable is it to be a blessing! How great was the promise made to Abraham, "In thee shall all the families of the earth be blessed!"

VI. For us to follow the good example of the apostle Paul, would be the way for us to die as he did.

See, 2 Tim. 4:6–8:

> For I am now ready to be offered, and the time of my departure is at hand. I have fought a good fight, I have finished my course, I have kept the faith; henceforth there is laid up for me a crown of righteousness, which the Lord, the righteous Judge, shall give me at that day.

VII. This would secure us a distinguished crown of glory hereafter.

It is thought by some, and not without great probability, that the apostle Paul is the very next in glory to the man Jesus Christ himself. This is probable from his having done more good than any, and from his having done it though so great labors and sufferings. The apostle tells us, "Every man shall receive his own reward according to his own labor."

I shall conclude with mentioning some things as encouragements for us to endeavor to follow the excellent example of this great apostle. Many may be ready to say that it is in vain for them to try. The apostle was a person so greatly distinguished, it is in vain for them to endeavor to be like him. But for your encouragement, consider,

1. *That the apostle was a man of like passions with us.* He had naturally the same heart, the same corruptions, was under the same circumstances, the same guilt, and the same condemnation. There is this circumstance that attends the apostle's example to encourage us to endeavor to imitate him, which did not attend the example of Christ. And yet we are called upon to imitate the example of Christ. This is probably one main reason why not only the example of Christ, but also those of mere men, are set before us in

the Scriptures. Though you may think you have no great reason to hope to come up to the apostle's degree, yet that is no reason why you should not make his good example your pattern, and labor, as far as in you lies, to copy after him.

2. *This apostle, before he was converted, was a very wicked man, and a vile persecutor.* He often speaks of it himself. He sinned against great light.

3. *He had much greater hindrances and impediments to eminent holiness from without than any of us have.* His circumstances made it more difficult for him.

4. *The same God, the same Savior, and the same head of divine influence are ready to help our sincere endeavors, that helped him.*

Let us therefore not excuse ourselves, but in good earnest endeavor to follow so excellent an example. And then, however weak we are in ourselves, we may hope to experience Christ's support, and be able to say from our own experience, as the apostle did before him, "when I am weak, then am I strong."

The Manner in which the Salvation of the Soul is to be Sought

September 1740.

"Thus did Noah; according to all that God commanded him, so did he."—*Genesis 6:22*

C oncerning these words, I would observe three things:

- *What [was] it that God commanded Noah, to which these words refer?* It was the building of an ark according to the particular direction of God, against the time when the flood of waters should come; and the laying up of food for himself, his family, and the other animals, which were to be preserved in the ark. We have the particular commands which God gave him respecting this affair, from the 14th verse, "Make thee an ark of gopher wood."

- *We may observe the special design of the work which God had enjoined upon Noah:* it was to save himself and his family, when the rest of the world should be drowned. See ver. 17, 18.

- *We may observe Noah's obedience.* He obeyed God: thus did Noah. And his obedience was thorough and universal: according to all that God commanded him, so did he. He not only began, but he went through his work, which God had commanded him to undertake for his salvation from the flood. To this obedience the apostle refers in Heb. 11:7, "By faith, Noah, being warned of God of things not seen as yet, moved with fear, prepared an ark to the saving of his house."

Doctrine

We should be willing to engage in and go through great undertakings, in order to gain our own salvation.

The building of the ark, which was enjoined upon Noah, that he and his family might be saved, was a great undertaking: the ark was a building of vast size; the length of it being three hundred cubits, the breadth of it fifty cubits, and the height of it thirty cubits. A cubit, till of late, was by learned men reckoned to be equal to a foot and a half of our measure. But lately some learned men of our nation have traveled into Egypt, and other ancient countries, and have measured some ancient buildings there, which are of several thousand years standing, and of which ancient histories give us the dimensions in cubits; particularly the pyramids of Egypt, which are standing entire at this day. By measuring these, and by comparing the measure in feet with the ancient accounts of their measure in cubits, a cubit is found to be almost two and twenty inches. Therefore learned men more lately reckon a cubit much larger than they did formerly. So that the ark, reckoned so much larger every way, will appear to be almost of double the bulk which was formerly ascribed to it. According to this computation of the cubit, it was more than five hundred and fifty feet long, about ninety feet broad, and about fifty feet in height.*

To build such a structure, with all those apartments and divisions in it which were necessary, and in such a manner as to be fit to float upon the water for so long a time, was then a great undertaking. It took Noah, with all the workmen he employed, a hundred and twenty years, or thereabouts, to build it. For so long it was, that the Spirit of God strove, and the long-suffering God waited on the old world, as you may see in Gen. 4:3: "My Spirit shall I not always strive with man; yet his days shall be a hundred and twenty years." All this while the ark was a-preparing, as appears by 1 Pet. 3:20: "When once the long-suffering of God waited in the days of Noah,

---

* In Edwards' time, the latest scholarly research pointed to this new, larger measurement for a cubit. Modern calculations, however, have returned to the earlier concept, and calculate that a cubit is the originally understood 18 inches, or 46 cm.

while the ark was a-preparing." It was a long time that Noah constantly employed himself in this business. Men would esteem that undertaking very great, which should keep them constantly employed even for one half of that time. Noah must have had a great and constant care upon his mind for these one hundred and twenty years, in superintending this work, and in seeing that all was done exactly according to the directions which God had given him.

Not only was Noah himself continually employed, but it required a great number of workmen to be constantly employed, during all that time, in procuring, and collecting, and fitting the materials, and in putting them together in due form. How great a thing was it for Noah to undertake such a work! For beside the continual care and labor, it was a work of vast expense. It is not probable that any of that wicked generation would put to a finger to help forward such a work, which doubtless they believed was merely the fruit of Noah's folly, without full wages. Noah must needs have been very rich, to be able to bear the expense of such a work, and to pay so many workmen for so long a time. It would have been a very great expense for a prince; and doubtless Noah was very rich, as Abraham and Job were afterwards. But it is probable that Noah spent all his worldly substance in this work, thus manifesting his faith in the word of God, by selling all he had, as believing there would surely come a flood, which would destroy all; so that if he should keep what he had, it would be of no service to him. Herein he has set us an example, showing us how we ought to sell all for our salvation.

Noah's undertaking was of great difficulty, as it exposed him to the continual reproaches of all his neighbors, for that whole one hundred and twenty years. None of them believed what he told them of a flood which was about to drown the world. For a man to undertake such a vast piece of work, under the notion that it should be the means of saving him when the world should be destroyed—it made him the continual laughing-stock of the world. When he was about to hire workmen, doubtless all laughed at him, and we may suppose, that though the workmen consented to work for wages, yet they laughed at the folly of him who employed them. When the ark was begun, we may suppose that every one that passed by and saw such a huge bulk stand there, laughed at, it, calling it "Noah's folly."

In these days, men are with difficulty brought to do or submit to that which makes them the objects of the reproach of all their neighbors. Indeed, if while some reproach them, others stand by them and honor them, this will support them. But it is very difficult for a man to go on in a way wherein he makes himself the laughing stock of the whole world, and wherein he can find none who do not despise him. Where is the man that can stand the shock of such a trial for one hundred and twenty years?

But in such an undertaking as this, Noah, at the divine direction, engaged and went through it, that himself and his family might be saved from the common destruction which was shortly about to come on the world. He began, and also made an end: "According to all that God commanded him, so did he." Length of time did not weary him: he did not grow weary of his vast expense. He stood the shock of the derision of all his neighbors; and of all the world year after year: he did not grow weary of being their laughing-stock, so as to give over his enterprise; but persevered in it till the ark was finished. After this, he was at the trouble and charge of procuring stores for the maintenance of his family, and of all the various kinds of creatures, for so long a time. Such an undertaking he engaged in and went through in order to [obtain] a *temporal* salvation. How great an undertaking then should men be willing to engage in and go through in order to their *eternal* salvation! A salvation from an eternal deluge; from being overwhelmed with the billows of God's wrath, of which Noah's flood was but a shadow.

I shall particularly handle this doctrine under the three following propositions.

> I. There is a work or business which must be undertaken and accomplished by men, if they would be saved.
>
> II. This business is a great undertaking.
>
> III. Men should be willing to enter upon and go through this undertaking though it be great, seeing it is for their own salvation.

I. *Proposition.* There is a work or business which men must enter upon and accomplish, in order to their salvation.

Men have no reason to expect to be saved in idleness, or to go to heaven in a way of doing nothing. No; in order to it, there is a great work, which must be not only begun, but finished. I shall speak upon this proposition, in answer to two inquiries.

Inquiry 1. What is this work or business which must be undertaken and accomplished in order to the salvation of men?

Answer. It is the work of seeking salvation in a way of constant observance of all the duty to which God directs us in his word. If we would be saved, we must seek salvation. For although men do not obtain heaven of themselves; they do not go thither accidentally, or without any intention or endeavors of their own. God, in his word, hath directed men to seek their salvation as they would hope to obtain it. There is a race that is set before them, which they must run, and in that race, come off victors, in order to their winning the prize.

The Scriptures have told us what particular duties must be performed by us in order to gain our salvation. It is not sufficient that men seek their salvation only in the observance of *some* of those duties; but they must be observed universally. The work we have to do is not an obedience only to some, but to *all* the commands of God; a compliance with every institution of worship; a diligent use of all the appointed means of grace; a doing of all duty towards God and towards man. It is not sufficient that men have some respect to all the commands of God, and that they may be said to seek their salvation in some sort of observance of all the commands; but they must be *devoted* to it.

They must not make this a business by the by, or a thing in which they are negligent and careless, or which they do with a slack hand; but it must be their great business, being attended to as their great concern. They must not only seek, but strive; they must do what their hand findeth to do with their might, as men thoroughly engaged in their minds, and influenced and set forward by great desire and strong resolution. They must act as those that see so much of the importance of religion above all other things, that every thing else must be as an occasional affair, and nothing must stand in competition with its duties. This must be the one thing they do; Phil. 3:13, "This one thing I do." It must be the business to which they make all other affairs give place, and to which they are ready to make other things a sacrifice. They must be ready to part with pleasures and honor, estate and life, and to sell all, that they may successfully accomplish this business.

It is required of every man, that he not only do something in this business, but that he should devote himself to it; which implies that he should give up himself to it, all his affairs, and all his temporal enjoyments. This is the import of taking up the cross, of taking Christ's yoke upon us, and of denying ourselves to follow Christ. The rich young man, who came kneeling to Christ to know what he should do to be saved, Mark 10:17, in some sense sought salvation, but did not obtain it. In some sense he kept all the commands from his youth up; but was not cordially devoted to this business. He had not made a sacrifice to it of all his enjoyments, as appeared when Christ came to try him; he would not part with his estate for him.

It is not only necessary that men should seem to be very much engaged, and appear as if they were devoted to their duty for a little while; but there must be a constant devotedness, in a persevering way, as Noah was to the business of the building the ark, going on with that great, difficult, and expensive affair, till it was finished, and till the flood came. Men must not only be diligent in the use of the means of grace, and be anxiously engaged to escape eternal ruin, till they obtain hope and comfort; but afterwards they must persevere in the duties of religion, till the flood come, the flood of death. Not only must the faculties, strength, and possessions of men be devoted to this work, but also their time and their lives; they must give up their whole lives to it, even to the very day when God causes the storms and floods to come. This is the work or business which men have to do in order to [gain] their salvation.

Inquiry 2. Why is it needful that men should undertake to go through such a work in order to gain their salvation?

Answer 1. Not to merit salvation, or to recommend them to the saving mercy of God. Men are not saved on the account of any work of theirs, and yet they are not saved without works. If we merely consider what it is for which, or on the account of which, men are saved, no work at all in men is necessary to their salvation. In this respect they are saved wholly without any work of theirs: Tit. 3:5, "Not by works of righteousness which we have done, but according to his mercy he saved us, by the washing of regeneration, and renewing of the Holy Ghost." We must indeed be saved on the account of works; but not our own. It is on account of the works which Christ hath done for us. Works are the fixed price of eternal life; it is fixed by an eternal, unalterable rule of righteousness. But since the fall there is no hope of our doing these works, without salvation offered freely without money and without price. But,

Answer 2. Though it be not needful that we do anything to merit salvation, which Christ hath fully merited for all who believe in him; yet God, for wise and holy ends, hath appointed, that we should come to final salvation in no other way, but that of good works done by us. God did not save Noah on account of the labor and expense he was at in building the ark. Noah's salvation from the flood was an instance of the free and distinguishing mercy of God. Nor did God stand in need of Noah's care, or cost, or labor, to build an ark. The same power which created the world, and which brought the flood of waters upon the earth, could have made the ark in an instant, without any care or cost to Noah, or any of the labor of those workmen who were employed for so long a time. Yet God was pleased to appoint, that Noah should be saved in this way. So God hath appointed that man should not be saved without his undertaking and doing this work of which I have been speaking; and therefore we are commanded "to work out our own salvation with fear and trembling," Philip. 2:12.

There are many wise ends to be answered by the establishment of such a work as prerequisite to salvation. The glory of God requires it. For although God stand in no need of anything that men do to recommend them to his saving mercy, yet it would reflect much on the glory of God's wisdom and holiness, to bestow salvation on men in such a way as tends to encourage them in sloth and wickedness; or in any other way than that which tends to promote diligence and holiness. Man was made capable of action, with many powers of both body and mind fitting him for it. He was made for business and not idleness, and the main business for which he was made was that of religion. Therefore it becomes the wisdom of God to bestow salvation and happiness on man in such a way as tends most to promote his end in this respect, and to stir him up to a diligent use of his faculties and talents.

It becomes the wisdom of God so to order it, that things of great value and importance should not be obtained without great labor and diligence. Much human learning and great moral accomplishments are not to be obtained without care and labor. It is wisely so ordered, in order to maintain in man a due sense of the value of those things which are excellent. If great things were in common easily obtained, it would have a tendency to cause men to slight and undervalue them. Men commonly despise those things which are cheap, and which are obtained without difficulty.

Although the work of obedience performed by men, be not necessary in order to merit salvation; yet it is necessary in order to their being prepared for it. Men cannot be prepared for salvation without seeking it in such a way as hath been described. This is necessary in order that they have a proper sense of their own necessities, and unworthiness; and in order that they be prepared and disposed to prize salvation when bestowed, and be properly thankful to God for it. The requisition of so great a work in order to our salvation is no way inconsistent with the freedom of the offer of salvation; as, after all, it is both offered and bestowed without any respect to our work, as the price or meritorious cause of our salvation, as I have already explained. Besides, salvation bestowed in this way is better for us, more for our advantage and happiness both in this and the future world, than if it were given without this requisition.

II. *Proposition.* **This work or business, which must be done in order to the salvation of men, is a great undertaking.**

It often appears so to men upon whom it is urged. Utterly to break off from all their sins, and to give up themselves forever to the business of religion, without making a reserve of any one lust, submitting to and complying with every command of God, in all cases, and persevering therein, appears to many so great a thing, that they are in vain urged to undertake it. In so doing it seems to them, that they should give up themselves to a perpetual bondage. The greater part of men therefore choose to put it off, and keep it at as great a distance as they can. They cannot bear to think of entering immediately on such a hard service, and rather than do it, they will run the risk of eternal damnation, by putting it off to an uncertain future opportunity.

Although the business of religion is far from really being as it appears to such men, or the devil will be sure, if he can, to represent it in false colors to sinners, and make it appear as black and as terrible as he can; yet it is indeed a great business, a great undertaking, and it is fit that all who are urged to it should count the cost beforehand, and be sensible of the difficulty attending it. For though the devil discourages many from this undertaking, by representing it to be more difficult than it really is; yet with others he takes a contrary course and flatters them it is a very easy thing, a trivial business, which may be done at any time when they please, and so emboldens them to defer it from that consideration. But let none conceive any other notion of that business of religion, which is absolutely necessary to their salvation, than that it is a great undertaking. It is so on the following accounts.

1. *It is a business of great labor and care.* There are many commands to be obeyed, many duties to be done, duties to God, duties to our neighbor, and duties to ourselves. There is much opposition in the way of these duties from without. There is a subtle and powerful adversary laying all manner of blocks in the way. There are innumerable temptations of Satan to be resisted and repelled. There is great opposition from the world, innumerable snares laid, on every side, many rocks and mountains to be passed over, many streams to be passed through, and many flatteries and enticements from a vain world to be resisted. There is a great opposition from within; a dull and sluggish heart, which is exceedingly averse from that activity in religion which is necessary; a carnal heart, which is averse from religion and spiritual exercises, and continually drawing the contrary way; and a proud and a deceitful heart, in which corruption will be exerting itself in all

manner of ways. So that nothing can be done to any effect without a most strict and careful watch, great labor and strife.

2. *It is a constant in business.* In that business which requires great labor, men love now and then to have a space of relaxation, that they may rest from their extraordinary labor. But this is a business which must be followed every day. Luke 9:23, "If any man will come after me, let him deny himself, and take up his cross daily and follow me." We must never give ourselves any relaxation from this business; it must be continually prosecuted day after day. If sometimes we make a great stir and bustle concerning religion, but then lay all aside to take our ease, and do so from time to time, it will be of no good effect; we had even as good do nothing at all. The business of religion so followed is never like to come to any good issue, nor is the work ever like to be accomplished to any good purpose.

3. *It is a great undertaking, as it is an undertaking of great expense.* We must, therein sell all: we must follow this business at the expense of all our unlawful pleasures and delights, at the expense of our carnal ease, often at the expense of our substance, of our credit among men, the good will of our neighbors, at the expense of all our earthly friends, and even at the expense of life itself. Herein it is like Noah's undertaking to build the ark, which, as hath been shown was a costly undertaking: it was expensive to his reputation among men, exposing him to be the continual laughing-stock of all his neighbors and of the whole world: and it was expensive to his estate, and probably cost him all that he had.

4. *Sometimes the fear, trouble, and exercise of mind which are undergone respecting this business, and the salvation of the soul, are great and long continued, before any comfort is obtained.* Sometimes persons in this situation labor long in the dark, and sometimes, as it were, in the very fire, they having great distress of conscience, great fears, and many perplexing temptations, before they obtain light and comfort to make their care and labor more easy to them. They sometimes earnestly, and for a long time, seek comfort, but find it not, because they seek it not in a right manner, nor in the right objects. God therefore hides his face. They cry, but God doth not answer their prayers. They strive, but all seems in vain. They seem to themselves not at all to get forward, or nearer to a deliverance from sin: but to go backward, rather than forward. They see no glimmerings of light: things rather appear darker and darker. Insomuch that they are often ready to be discouraged, and to sink under the weight of their present distress, and under the prospect of future misery. In this situation, and under these views, some are almost driven to despair. Many, after they have

obtained some saving comfort, are again involved in darkness and trouble. It is with them as it was with the Christian Hebrews, Heb. 10:32, "After ye were illuminated, ye endured a great fight of afflictions." Some through a melancholy habit and distemper of body, together with Satan's temptations, spend a great part of their lives in distress and darkness, even after they have had some saving comfort.

5. *It is a business which, by reason of the many difficulties, snares, and dangers that attend it, requires much instruction, consideration, and counsel.* There is no business wherein men stand in need of counsel more than in this. It is a difficult undertaking, a hard matter to proceed aright in it. There are ten thousand wrong ways, which men may take; there are many labyrinths wherein many poor souls are entangled and never find the way out; there are many rocks on which thousands of souls have suffered shipwreck, for want of having steered aright.

Men of themselves know not how to proceed in this business, any more than the children of Israel in the wilderness knew where to go without the guidance of the pillar of cloud and fire. There is great need that they search the Scriptures, and give diligent heed to the instructions and directions contained in them, as to a light shining in a dark place, and that they ask counsel of those skilled in these matters. And there is no business in which men have so much need of seeking to God by prayer, for his counsel, and that he would lead them in the right way, and show them the strait gate. "For strait is the gate and narrow is the way which leadeth unto life, and few there be that find it"; yea, there are none that find it without direction from heaven. The building of the ark was a work of great difficulty on this account, that Noah's wisdom was not sufficient to direct him how to make such a building as should be a sufficient security against such a flood, and which should be a convenient dwelling-place for himself, his family, and all the various kinds of beasts and birds, and creeping things. Nor could he ever have known how to construct this building, had not God directed him.

6. *This business never ends till life ends.* They that undertake this laborious, careful, expensive, self-denying business, must not expect to rest from their labors, till death shall have put an end to them. The long continuance of the work which Noah undertook was what especially made it a great undertaking. This also was what made the travel of the children of Israel through the wilderness appear so great to them, that it was continued for so long a time. Their spirits failed, they were discouraged, and

had not a heart to go through with so great an undertaking. But such is this business that it runs parallel with life, whether it be longer or shorter. Although we should live to a great age, our race and warfare will not be finished till death shall come. We must not expect that an end will be put to our labor, and care, and strife, by any hope of a good estate which we may obtain. Past attainments and past success will not excuse us from what remains for the future, nor will they make future constant labor and care unnecessary to our salvation.

III. *Proposition*: **Men should be willing to engage in and go through this business, however great and difficult it may seem to them, seeing it is for their own salvation. Because:**

1. *A deluge of wrath will surely come.* The inhabitants of the old world would not believe that there would come such a flood of waters upon the earth as that of which Noah told them, though he told them often; neither would they take any care to avoid the destruction. Yet such a deluge did come; nothing of all those things of which Noah had forewarned them, failed.

So there will surely come a more dreadful deluge of divine wrath on this wicked world. We are often forewarned of it in the Scriptures, and the world, as then, doth not believe any such thing. Yet the threatening will as certainly be accomplished, as the threatening denounced against the old world. A day of wrath is coming; it will come at its appointed season; it will not tarry, it shall not be delayed one moment beyond its appointed time.

2. *All such as do not seasonably undertake and go through the great work mentioned will surely be swallowed up in this deluge.* When the floods of wrath shall come, they will universally overwhelm the wicked world: all such as shall not have taken care to prepare an ark, will surely be swallowed up in it; they will find no other way of escape. In vain shall salvation be expected from the hills, and from the multitude of mountains; for the flood shall be above the tops of all the mountains. Or if they shall hide themselves in the caves and dens of the mountains, there the waters of the flood will find them out, and there shall they miserably perish. As those of the old world who were not in the ark perished, Gen. 7:21, 23, so all who shall not have secured to themselves a place in the spiritual ark of the gospel, shall perish much more miserably than the old world. Doubtless the inhabitants of the old world had many contrivances to save themselves. Some, we may suppose, ascended to the tops of their houses,

being driven out of one story to another, till at last they perished. Others climbed to the tops of high towers; who yet were washed thence by the boisterous waves of the rising flood. Some climbed to the tops of trees; others to the tops of mountains, and especially of the highest mountains. But all was in vain; the flood sooner or later swallowed them all up; only Noah and his family, who had taken care to prepare an ark, remained alive. So it will doubtless be at the end of the world, when Christ shall come to judge the world in righteousness. Some, when they shall look up and see him coming in the clouds of heaven, shall hide themselves in closets, and secret places in their houses. Others, flying to the caves and dens of the earth, shall attempt to hide themselves there. Others shall call upon the rocks and mountains to fall on them, and cover them from the face of him that sitteth on the throne, and from the wrath of the Lamb. So it will be after the sentence is pronounced, and wicked men see that terrible fire coming, which is to burn this world forever, and which will be a deluge of fire, and will burn the earth even to the bottoms of the mountains, and to its very center. Deut. 32:22,

> For a fire is kindled in mine anger, and shall burn to the lowest Hell, and shall consume the earth with her increase, and set on fire the foundations of the mountains.

I say, when the wicked shall, after the sentence, see this great fire beginning to kindle, and to take hold of this earth; there will be many contrivances devised by them to escape, some flying to caves and holes in the earth, some hiding themselves in one place, and some in another. But let them hide themselves where they will, or let them do what they will, it will be utterly in vain. Every cave shall burn as an oven, the rocks and mountains shall melt with fervent heat, and if they could creep down to the very center of the earth, still the heat would follow them, and rage with as much vehemence there, as on the very surface.

So when wicked men, who neglect their great work in their lifetime, who are not willing to go through the difficulty and labor of this work, draw near to death, they sometimes do many things to escape death, and put forth many endeavors to lengthen out their lives at least a little longer. For this end, they send for physicians, and perhaps many are consulted, and their prescriptions are punctually observed. They also use many endeavors to save their souls from Hell. They cry to God; they confess their past sins; they promise future reformation; and, oh what would they not give for some small addition to their lives, or some hope of future happiness! But all proves in vain: God hath numbered their days and finished them; and as they have sinned away the day of grace, they must even bear the consequence, and forever lie down in sorrow.

3. *The destruction, when it shall come, will be infinitely terrible.* The destruction of the old world by the flood was terrible; but that eternal destruction which is coming on the wicked is infinitely more so. That flood of waters was but an image of this awful flood of divine vengeance. When the waters poured down, more like spouts or cataracts, or the fall of a great river, than like rain; what an awful appearance was there of the wrath of God! This however, is but an image of that terrible outpouring of the wrath of God which shall be forever, yea forever and ever, on wicked men. And when the fountains of the great deep were broken up, and the waters burst forth out of the ground though they had issued out of the womb (Job 38:8), this was an image of the mighty breakings forth of God's wrath, which shall be, when the flood gates of wrath shall be drawn up. How may we suppose that the wicked of the old world repented that they had not hearkened to the warnings which Noah had given them, when they saw these dreadful things, and saw that they must perish! How much more will you repent your refusing to hearken to the gracious warnings of the gospel, when you shall see the fire of God's wrath against you, pouring down from heaven, and bursting on all sides out of bowels of the earth!

4. *Though the work which is necessary in order to man's salvation be a great work, yet it is not impossible.* What was required of Noah, doubtless appeared a very great and difficult undertaking. Yet he undertook it with resolution, and he was carried through it. So if we undertake this work with the same good will and resolution, we shall undoubtedly be successful. However difficult it be, yet multitudes have gone through it, and have obtained salvation by the means. It is not a work beyond the faculties of our nature, nor beyond the opportunities which God giveth us. If men will but take warning, and hearken to counsel, if they will but be sincere and in good earnest, be seasonable in their work, take their opportunities, use their advantages be steadfast, and not wavering; they shall not fail.

Application

The use I would make of this doctrine, is to exhort all to undertake and go through this great work, which they have to do in order to their salvation, and this, let [although] the work seem ever so great and difficult. If your nature be averse to it, and there seems to be very frightful things in the way, so that your heart is ready to fail at the prospect; yet seriously consider what has been said, and act a wise part. Seeing it is for yourselves, for your own salvation; seeing it is for so great a salvation, for your deliverance from eternal destruction; and seeing it is of such absolute necessity in order to your salvation, that the deluge of divine wrath will come, and there will be no escaping it without preparing an ark; is it not best for you to undertake the work, engage in it with your might, and go through it, though this cannot be done without great labor, care, and difficulty, and expense?

I would by no means flatter you concerning this work, or go about to make you believe, that you shall find an easy light business of it: no, I would not have you expect any such thing. I would have you sit down and count the cost; and if you cannot find it in your hearts to engage in a great, hard, laborious, and expensive undertaking, and to persevere in it to the end of life, pretend not to be religious. Indulge yourselves in your ease; follow your pleasures; eat, drink, and be merry; even conclude to go to Hell in that way, and never make any more pretenses of seeking your salvation.

Here consider several things in particular.

1. How often you have been warned of the approaching flood of God's wrath? How frequently you have been told of Hell, heard the threatenings of the word of God set before you, and been warned to flee from the wrath to come? It is with you as it was with the inhabitants of the old world. Noah warned them abundantly of the approaching flood, and counseled them to take care for their safety, 1 Pet. 3:19, 20. Noah warned them in words; and he preached to them. He warned them also in his actions. His building the ark, which took him so long a time, and in which he employed so many hands, was a standing warning to them. All the blows of the hammer and axe, during the progress of that building, were so many calls and warnings to the old world, to take care for their preservation from the approaching destruction. Every knock of the workmen was a knock of Jesus Christ at the door of their hearts: but they would not hearken. All these warnings, though repeated every day, and continued for so long a time, availed nothing.

Now, is it not much so with you, as it was with them? How often have you been warned! How have you heard the warning knocks of the gospel, Sabbath after Sabbath, for these many years! Yet how have some of you no more regarded them than the inhabitants of the old world regarded the noise of the workmen's tools in Noah's ark!

Objection: But here possibly it may be objected by some, that though it be true they have often been told of Hell, yet they never saw anything of it, and therefore they cannot realize it that there is any such place. They have often heard of Hell, and are told that wicked men, when they die, go to a most dreadful place of torment; that hereafter there will be a day of judgment, and that the world will be consumed by fire. But how do they know that it is really so? How do they know what becomes of those wicked men that die? None of them come back to tell them. They have nothing to depend on but the word which they hear. And how do they know that all is not a cunningly-devised fable?

Answer. The sinners of the old world had the very same objection against what Noah told them of a flood about to drown the world. Yet the bare word of God proved to be sufficient evidence that such a thing was coming. What was the reason that none of the many millions then upon earth believed what Noah said, but this, that it was a strange thing, that no such thing had ever before been known? And what a strange story must that of Noah have appeared to them, wherein he told them of a deluge of waters above the tops of the mountains! Therefore it is said, Heb. 11:7, that "Noah was warned of God of things not seen as yet." It is probable, none could conceive how it could be that the whole world should be drowned in a flood of waters; and all were ready to ask, where there was water enough for it; and by what means it should be brought upon the earth. Noah did not tell them how it should be brought to pass; he only told them that God had said that it should be: and that proved to be enough. The event showed their folly in not depending on the mere word of God, who was able, who knew how to bring it to pass, and who could not lie.

In like manner the word of God will prove true, in threatening a flood of eternal wrath to overwhelm all the wicked. You will believe it when the event shall prove it, when it shall be too late to profit by the belief. The word of God will never fail; nothing is so sure as that: heaven and earth shall pass away, but the word of God shall not pass away. It is firmer than mountains of brass. At the end, the vision will speak and not lie. The decree shall bring forth, and all wicked men shall know that God is the Lord, that he is a God of truth, and that they are fools who will not depend on his word. The wicked of the old world counted Noah a fool for depending so much on the word of God, as to put himself to all the fatigue and expense of building the ark; but the event showed that they themselves were the fools, and that he was wise.

2. Consider that the Spirit of God will not always strive with you; nor will his long suffering always wait upon you. So God said concerning the inhabitants of the old world, Gen. 4:3: "My Spirit shall not always strive with man, for that he also is flesh; yet his days shall be a hundred and twenty years." All this while God was striving with them. It was a day of grace with them, and God's long-suffering all this while waited upon them: 1 Peter 3:20, "Which sometime were disobedient, when once the long-suffering of God waited in the days of Noah, while the ark was a preparing." All this while they had an opportunity to escape, if they would but hearken and believe God. Even after the ark was finished, which seems to have been but little before the flood came, still there was an opportunity; the door of the ark stood open for some time. There was some time during which Noah was employed in laying up stores in the ark. Even then it was not too late; the door of the ark yet stood open. About a week before the flood came, Noah was com- manded to begin to gather in the beasts and birds. During this last week still the door of the ark stood open. But on the very day that the flood began to come, while the rain was yet withheld, Noah and his wife, his three sons, and their wives, went into the ark; and we are told, Gen. 7:16, that "God shut him in." Then the day of God's patience was past; the door of the ark was shut; God himself, who shuts and no man opens, shut the door. Then all hope of their escaping the flood was past; it was too late to repent that they had not hearkened to Noah's warnings, and had not entered into the ark while the door stood open.

After Noah and his family had entered into the ark, and God had shut them in, after the windows of heaven were opened, and they saw how the waters were poured down out of heaven, we may suppose that many of those who were near came running to the door of the ark, knocking, and crying most piteously for entrance. But it was too late; God himself had shut the door, and Noah had no license, and probably no power, to open it. We may suppose, they stood knocking and calling," Open to us, open to us; O let us in; we beg that we may be let in." And probably some of them pleaded old acquaintance with Noah; that they had always been his neigh- bors, and had even helped him to build the ark. But all was in vain. There they stood till the waters of the flood came, and without mercy swept them away from the door of the ark.

So it will be with you, if you continue to refuse to hearken to the warnings which are given you. Now God is striving with you; now he is warning you of the approaching flood, and calling upon you Sabbath af- ter Sabbath. Now the door of the ark stands open. But God's Spirit will not always strive with you; his long-suffering will not always wait upon you. There is an appointed day of God's patience, which is as certainly limited as it was to the old world. God hath set your bounds, which you cannot pass. Though now warnings are continued in plenty, yet there will be last knocks and last calls, the last that ever you shall hear. When the appointed time shall be elapsed, God will shut the door, and you shall never see it open again; for God shutteth, and no man openeth. If you improve not your opportunity before that time, you will cry in vain, "Lord, Lord, open to us," Matt. 25:11, and Luke 23:25, etc. While you shall stand at the door with your piteous cries, the flood of God's wrath will come upon you, overwhelm you, and you shall not escape. The tempest shall carry you away without mercy, and you shall be forever swallowed up and lost.

3. Consider how mighty the billows of divine wrath will be when they shall come. The waters of Noah's flood were very great. The deluge was vast; it was very deep; the billows reached fifteen cubits above the highest mountains; and it was an ocean which had no shore; signifying the greatness of that wrath which is coming on wicked men in another world, which will be like a mighty flood of waters overwhelming them, and rising vastly high over their heads, with billows reaching to the very heavens. Those billows will be higher and heavier than mountains on their poor souls. The wrath of God will be an ocean without shores, as Noah's flood was: it will be misery that will have no end. The misery of the damned in Hell can be better represented by nothing, than by a deluge of misery, a mighty deluge of wrath, which will be ten thousand times worse than a deluge of waters; for it will be a deluge of liquid fire, as in the Scriptures it is called a lake of fire and brimstone. At the end of the world all the wicked shall be swallowed up in a vast deluge of fire, which shall be as great and as mighty as Noah's deluge of water. See 2 Pet. 3:5, 6, 7. After that the wicked will have mighty billows of fire and brimstone eternally rolling over their poor souls, and their miserable tormented bodies. Those billows may be called vast liquid mountains of fire and brimstone. And when one billow shall have gone over their heads, another shall follow, without intermission, giving them no rest day nor night to all eternity.

4. This flood of wrath will probably come upon you suddenly, when you all think little of it, and it shall seem far from you. So the flood came upon the old world. See Matt. 24:36, etc. Probably many of them were surprised in the night by the waters bursting suddenly in at their doors, or under the foundations of their houses, coming in upon them in their beds. For when the fountains of the great deep were broken up, the waters, as observed before, burst forth in mighty torrents. To such a sudden surprise of the wicked of the old world in the night, probably that alludes in Job 27:20, "Terrors take hold on him as waters; a tempest stealeth him away in the night." So destruction is wont to come on wicked men, who hear many warnings of approaching destruction, and yet will not be influenced by them. For "he that is often reproved, and hardeneth his neck, shall suddenly be destroyed, and that without remedy," Prov. 29:1. And "when they shall say, 'Peace and safety'; then sudden destruction cometh upon them, as travail upon a woman with child, and they shall not escape" (1 Thess. 5:3).

5. *If you will not hearken to the many warnings which are given you of approaching destruction, you will be guilty of more than brutish madness.* "The ox knoweth his owner, and the ass his master's crib." They know upon whom they are dependent, and whom they must obey, and act accordingly. But you, so long as you neglect your own salvation, act as if you knew not God, your Creator and Proprietor, nor your dependence upon him. The very beasts, when they see signs of an approaching storm, will betake themselves to their dens for shelter. Yet you, when abundantly warned of the approaching storm of divine vengeance, will not fly to the hiding-place from the storm, and the covert from the tempest. The sparrow, the swallow, and other birds, when they are forewarned of approaching winter, will betake themselves to a safer climate. Yet you who have been often forewarned of the piercing blasts of divine wrath, will not, in order to escape them, enter into the New Jerusalem, of most mild and salubrious air, though the gate stands wide open to receive you. The very ants will be diligent in summer to lay up for winter: yet you will do nothing to lay up in store a good foundation against the time to come. Balaam's ass would not run upon a drawn sword, though his master, for the sake of gain, would expose himself to the sword of God's wrath; and so God made the dumb ass, both in words and actions, to rebuke the madness of the prophet, 1 Pet. 2:16. In like manner, you, although you have been oft warned that the sword of God's wrath is drawn against you, and will certainly be thrust through you, if you proceed in your present course, still proceed, regardless of the consequence.

So God made the very beasts and birds of the old world to rebuke the madness of the men of that day: for they, even all sorts of them, fled to the ark while the door was yet open: which the men of that day refused to do; God hereby, thus signifying, that their folly was greater than that of the very brute creatures. Such folly and madness are you guilty of; who refuse to hearken to the warnings that are given you of the approaching flood of the wrath of God.

You have been once more warned today, while the door of the ark yet stands open. You have, as it were, once again heard the knocks of the hammer and axe in the building of the ark, to put you in mind that a flood is approaching. Take heed therefore that you do not still stop your ears, treat these warnings with a regardless heart, and still neglect the great work which you have to do, lest the flood of wrath suddenly come upon you, sweep you away, and there be no remedy.

Hypocrites Deficient in the Duty of Prayer

September 1740.

"Will he always call upon God?"—Job 27:10

Concerning these words, I would observe:

- Who is it that is here spoken of, viz. the hypocrite? As you may see, if you take the two preceding verses with the verse of the text.

  For what is the hope of the hypocrite, though he hath gained, when God taketh away his soul? Will God bear his cry when trouble cometh upon him? Will he delight himself in the Almighty? Will he always call up on God?

  Job's three friends, in their speeches to him, insisted much upon it, that he was an hypocrite. But Job, in this chapter, asserts his sincerity and integrity, and shows how different his own behavior had been from that of hypocrite. Particularly he declares his steadfast and immoveable resolution of persevering and holding out in the ways of religion and righteousness to the end; as you may see in the six first verses. In the text, he shows how contrary to this steadfastness and perseverance the character of the hypocrite is, who is not wont thus to hold out in religion.

- We may observe what duty of religion it is, with respect to which the hypocrite is deciphered in the text, and that is the duty of prayer; or calling upon God.
- Here is something supposed of the hypocrite relating to this duty, viz. that he may continue in it for a while; he may call upon God for a season.
- Something asserted, viz. that it is not the manner of hypocrites to continue always in this duty. Will he always call upon God? It is in the form of an interrogation; but the words have the force of a strong negation, or of an assertion, that however the hypocrite may call upon God for a season, yet he will not always continue in it.

Doctrine

However hypocrites may continue for a season in the duty of prayer, yet it is their manner, after a while, in a great measure, to leave it off. In speaking upon this doctrine, I shall show,

I. How hypocrites often continue for a season to call upon God.

II. How it is their manner, after a while, in a great measure to leave off the practice of this duty.

III. Some reasons why this is the manner of hypocrites.

I. I would show how hypocrites often continue for a season in the duty of prayer.

1. *They do so for a while after they have received common illuminations and affections.* While they are under awakenings, they may, through fear of Hell, call upon God, and attend very constantly upon the duty of secret prayer. And after they have had some melting affections, having their hearts much moved with the goodness of God, or with some affecting encouragements, and false joy and comfort; while these impressions last they continue to call upon God in the duty of secret prayer.

2. After they have obtained a hope, and have made profession of their good estate, they often continue for a while in the duty of secret prayer. For a while they are affected with their hope: they think that God hath delivered them out of a natural condition, and given them an interest in Christ,

thus introducing them into a state of safety from that eternal misery which they lately feared. With this supposed kindness of God to them, they are much affected, and often find in themselves for a while a kind of love to God, excited by his supposed love to them. Now, while this affection towards God continues, the duties of religion seem pleasant to them; it is even with some delight that they approach to God in their closets; and for the present it may be, they think of no other than continuing to call upon God as long as they live.

Yea, they may continue in the duty of secret prayer for awhile after the liveliness of their affections is past, partly through the influence of their former intentions. They intended to continue seeking God always; and now suddenly to leave off, would therefore be too shocking to their own minds and partly through the force of their own preconceived notions, and what they have always believed, viz. that godly persons do continue in religion, and that their goodness is not like the morning cloud. Therefore, though they have no love to the duty of prayer, and begin to grow weary of it, yet as they love their own hope, they are somewhat backward to take a course, which will prove it to be a false hope, and so deprive them of it.

If they should at once carry themselves so as they have always been taught is a sign of a false hope, they would scare themselves. Their hope is dear to them, and it would scare them to see any plain evidence that it is not true. Hence, for a considerable time after the force of their illuminations and affections is over, and after they hate the duty of prayer, and would be glad to have done with it, if they could, without showing themselves to be hypocrites; they hold up a kind of attendance upon the duty of secret prayer. This may keep up the outside of religion in them for a good while, and occasion it to be somewhat slowly that they are brought to neglect it. They must not leave off suddenly, because that would be too great a shock to their false peace. But they must come gradually to it, as they find their consciences can bear it, and as they can find out devices and salvos to cover over the matter, and make their so doing consistent, in their own opinion, with the truth of their hope. But,

II. It is the manner of hypocrites, after a while, in a great measure to leave off the practice of this duty.

We are often taught, that the seeming goodness and piety of hypocrites is not of a lasting and persevering nature. It is so with respect to their practice of the duty of prayer in particular, and especially of secret prayer. They can omit this duty, and their omission of it not be taken notice of by others, who know what profession they have made. So that a regard to their own reputation doth not oblige them still to practice it. If others saw how they neglect it, it would exceedingly shock their charity towards them. But their neglect doth not fall under their observation; at least not under the observation of many. Therefore they may omit this duty, and still have the credit of being converted persons.

Men of this character can come to a neglect of secret prayer by degrees without very much shocking their peace. For though indeed for a converted person to live in a great measure without secret prayer, is very wide of the notion they once had of a true convert; yet they find means by degrees to alter their notions, and to bring their principles to suit with their inclinations; and at length they come to that, in their notions of things, that a man may be a convert, and yet live very much in neglect of this duty. In time, they can bring all things to suit well together, an hope of heaven, and an indulgence of sloth in gratifying carnal appetites, and living in a great measure a prayerless life. They cannot indeed suddenly make these things agree; it must be a work of time; and length of time will effect it. By degrees they find out ways to guard and defend their consciences against those powerful enemies; so that those enemies, and a quiet, secure conscience, can at length dwell pretty well together.

Whereas it is asserted in the doctrine, that it is the manner of hypocrites, after a while, in a great measure to leave off this duty; I would observe to you:

1. *That it is not intended but that they may commonly continue to the end of life in yielding an external attendance on open prayer, or prayer with others.* They may commonly be present at public prayers in the congregation, and also at family prayer. This, in such places of light as this is, men commonly do before ever they are so much as awakened. Many vicious persons, who make no pretense to serious religion, commonly attend public prayers in the congregation; and also more private prayers, in the families in which they live, unless it be when carnal designs interfere, or when their youthful pleasures and diversions, and their vain company call them; and then they make no conscience of attending family prayer. Otherwise they may continue to attend upon prayer as long as they live, and yet may truly be said not to call upon God. For such prayer, in the manner of it, is not their own. They are present only for the sake of their credit, or in compliance with others. They may be present at these prayers, and yet have no proper prayer of their

own. Many of those concerning whom it maybe said, as in Job 15:4, That they cast off fear and restrain prayer before God, are yet frequently present at family and public prayer.

2. But they in a great measure leave off the practice of secret prayer. They come to this pass by degrees. At first they begin to be careless about it, under some particular temptations. Because they have been out in young company, or have been taken up very much with worldly business, they omit it once: after that they more easily omit it again. Thus it presently becomes a frequent thing with them to omit it and after a while, it comes to that pass, that they seldom attend it. Perhaps they attend it on Sabbath days, and sometimes on other days. But they have ceased to make it a constant practice daily to retire to worship God alone, and to seek his face in secret places. They sometimes do a little to quiet conscience, and just to keep alive their old hope; because it would be shocking to them, even after all their subtle dealing with their consciences to call themselves converts, and yet totally to live without prayer. Yet the practice of secret prayer they have in a great measure left off.

I come now,

III. To the reasons why this is the manner of hypocrites.

1. Hypocrites never had the spirit of prayer given them. They may have been stirred up to the external performance of this duty, and that with a great deal of earnestness and affection, and yet always have been destitute of the true spirit of prayer. The spirit of prayer is a holy spirit, a gracious spirit. We read of the spirit of grace and supplication, Zech. 3:10. I will pour out on the house of David and the inhabitants of Jerusalem, the spirit of grace and supplications. Wherever there is a true spirit of supplication, there is the spirit of grace. The true spirit of prayer is no other than God's own Spirit dwelling in the hearts of the saints. And as this spirit comes from God, so doth it naturally tend to God in holy breathings and pantings. It naturally leads to God, to converse with him by prayer. Therefore the Spirit is said to make intercession for the saints with groanings which cannot be uttered, Rom. 8:26.

The Spirit of God makes intercession for them, as it is that Spirit which in some respect indites [dictates] their prayers, and leads them to pour out their souls before God. Therefore the saints are said to worship God in the spirit; Phil. 3:3. "We are the circumcision, who worship God in the Spirit;" and John 4:23. "The true worshipers worship the Father in spirit and in truth." The truly godly have the spirit of adoption, the spirit of a child, to which it is natural to go to God and call upon him, crying to him as to a father.

But hypocrites have nothing of this spirit of adoption: they have not the spirit of children; for this is a gracious and holy spirit, given only in a real work of regeneration. Therefore it is often mentioned as a part of the distinguishing character of the godly, that they call upon God. Psalm 145:18,19:

> The Lord is nigh to them that call upon him, to all that call upon him in truth. He will fulfil the desire of them that fear him; he will also hear their cry, and will save them.

Joel 2:32: "It shall come to pass, that whosoever calleth on the name of the Lord shall be saved."

It is natural to one who is truly born from above to pray to God, and to pour out his soul in holy supplications before his heavenly Father. This is as natural to the new nature and life as breathing is to the nature and life of the body. But hypocrites have not this new nature. Those illuminations and affections which they had, went away, and left no change of nature. Therefore prayer naturally dies away in them, having no foundation laid in the nature of the soul. It is maintained awhile only by a certain force put upon nature. But force is not constant; and as that declines, nature will take place again.

The spirit of a true convert is a spirit of true love to God, and that naturally inclines the soul to those duties wherein it is conversant with God, and makes it to delight in approaching him. But a hypocrite hath no such spirit. He is left under the reigning power of enmity against God, which naturally inclines him to shun his presence.

The spirit of a true convert is a spirit of faith and reliance on the power, wisdom, and mercy of God, and such a spirit is naturally expressed in prayer. True prayer is nothing else but faith expressed. Hence we read of the prayer of faith; James 5:15. True Christian prayer is the faith and reliance of the soul breathed forth in words. But a hypocrite is without the spirit of faith. He hath no true reliance or dependence on God, but is really self-dependent.

As to those common convictions and affections which the hypocrite had, and which made him keep up the duty of prayer for a while; [since] they [are] not reaching the bottom of the heart, nor being accompanied with any change of nature, a little thing extinguishes them. The cares of the world commonly choke and suffocate them, and often the pleasures and vanities of youth totally put an end to them, and with them ends their constant practice of the duty of prayer.

2. *When a hypocrite hath had his false conversion, his wants are, in his sense of things, already supplied, his desires are already answered, and so he finds no further business at the throne of grace.* He never was sensible that he had any other needs, but a need of being safe from hell. And now that he is converted, as he thinks, that need is supplied. Why then should he still go on to resort to the throne of grace with earnest requests? He is out of danger; all that he was afraid of is removed: he hath got enough to carry him to heaven, and what more should he desire?

While under awakenings, he had this to stir him up to go to God in prayer, that he was in continual fear of hell. This put him upon crying to God for mercy. But since in his own opinion he is converted, he hath no further business about which to go to God. And although he may keep up the duty of prayer in the outward form a little while, for fear of spoiling his hope, yet he will find it a dull business to continue it without necessity, and so by degrees he will let drop the practice. The work of the hypocrite is done when he is converted, and therefore he standeth in no further need of help.

But it is far otherwise with the true convert. His work is not done; but he finds still a great work to do, and great wants to be supplied. He sees himself still to be a poor, empty, helpless creature, and that he still stands in great and continual need of God's help. He is sensible that without God he can do nothing. A false conversion makes a man in his own eyes self-sufficient. He saith he is rich, and increased with goods, and hath need of nothing; and knoweth not that be is wretched, and miserable, and poor, and blind, and naked. But after a true conversion, the soul remains sensible of its own impotence and emptiness, as it is in itself, and its sense of it is rather increased than diminished. It is still sensible of its universal dependence on God for everything. A true convert is sensible that his grace is very imperfect; and he is very far from having all that he desires. Instead of that, by conversion are begotten in him new desires which he never had before. He now finds in him holy appetites, a hungering and thirsting after righteousness, a longing after more acquaintance and communion with God. So that he hath business enough still at the throne of grace; yea, his business there, instead of being diminished, is, since his conversion, rather increased.

3. *The hope which the hypocrite hath of his good estate takes off the force that the command of God before had upon his conscience; so that now he dares neglect so*

plain a duty. The command which requires the practice of the duty of prayer is exceeding plain; Matt. 26:41: "Watch and pray, that ye enter not into temptation." Eph. 6:18: "Praying always with all prayer and supplication in the spirit, and watching thereunto with all perseverance, and supplication for all saints." Matt. 6:6: "When thou prayest enter into thy closet, and when thou hast shut thy door, pray to thy Father which is in secret." As long as the hypocrite was in his own apprehension in continual danger of Hell, he durst not disobey these commands. But since he is, as he thinks, safe from Hell, he is grown bold, he dares to live in the neglect of the plainest command in the Bible.

4. *It is the manner of hypocrites, after a while, to return to sinful practices, which will tend to keep them from praying.* While they were under convictions, they reformed their lives, and walked very exactly. This reformation continues for a little time perhaps after their supposed conversion, while they are much affected with hope and false comfort. But as these things die away, their old lusts revive, and they by degrees return like the dog to his vomit, and the sow that was washed to her wallowing in the mire. They return to their sensual practices, to their worldly practices, to their proud and contentious practices, as before. And no wonder this makes them forsake their closets. Sinning and praying agree not well together. If a man be constant in the duty of secret prayer, it will tend to restrain him from willful sinning. So, on the other hand, if he allow himself in sinful practices, it will restrain him from praying. It will give quite another turn to his mind, so that he will have no disposition to the practice of such a duty. It will be contrary to him. A man who knows that he lives in sin against God, will not be inclined to come daily into the presence of God; but will rather be inclined to fly from his presence, as Adam, when he had eaten of the forbidden fruit, ran away from God, and hid himself among the trees of the garden.

To keep up the duty of prayer after he hath given loose to his lusts, would tend very much to disquiet a man's conscience. It would give advantage to his conscience to testify aloud against him. If he should come from his wickedness into the presence of God, immediately to speak to him, his conscience would, as it were; fly in his face. Therefore hypocrites, as they, by degrees, admit their wicked practices, exclude prayer.

5. *Hypocrites never counted the cost of perseverance in seeking God, and of following him to the end of life.* To continue instant in prayer with all perseverance to the end of life, requires much care, watchfulness, and labor. For much opposition is made to it by the flesh, the world, and the devil and

Christians meet with many temptations to forsake this practice. He that would persevere in this duty must be laborious in religion in general. But hypocrites never count the cost of such labor; i.e. they never were prepared in the disposition of their minds to give their lives to the service of God, and to the duties of religion. It is therefore no great wonder if they are weary and give out, after they have continued for a while, as their affections are gone, and they find that prayer to them grows irksome and tedious.

6. *Hypocrites have no interest in those gracious promises which God hath made to his people, of those spiritual supplies which are needful in order to uphold them in the way of their duty to the end.* God hath promised to true saints that they shall not forsake him; Jer. 32:40. I will put my fear into their hearts, that they shall not depart from me. He hath promised that he will keep them in the way of their duty; 1 Thess. 5:23, 24:

> And the God of peace sanctify you wholly. And I pray God your spirit, soul, and body, be preserved blameless unto the coming of our Lord Jesus Christ. Faithful is he that calleth you, who also will do it.

But hypocrites have no interest in these and such like promises, and therefore are liable to fall away. If God do[es] not uphold men, there is no dependence on their steadfastness. If the Spirit of God depart[s] from them, they will soon become careless and profane, and there will be an end to their seeming devotion and piety.

Application

The application may be in a use of *exhortation*, in two branches.

I. I would exhort those who have entertained a hope of their being true converts, and yet since their supposed conversion have left off the duty of secret prayer, and do ordinarily allow themselves in the omission of it, to throw away their hope.

If you have left off calling upon God, it is time for you to leave off hoping and flattering yourselves with an imagination that you are the children of God. Probably it will be a very difficult thing for you to do this. It is hard for a man to let go a hope of heaven, on which he hath once allowed himself to lay hold, and which he hath retained for a considerable time. True conversion is a rare thing; but that men are brought off from a false hope of conversion, after they are once settled and established in it, and have continued in it for some time, is much more rare.

Those things in men, which, if they were known to others, would be sufficient to convince others that they are hypocrites, will not convince themselves; and those things which would be sufficient to convince them concerning others, and to cause them to cast others entirely out of their charity, will not be sufficient to convince them concerning themselves. They can make larger allowances for themselves than they can for others. They can find out ways to solve objections against their own hope, when they can find none in the like case for their neighbor.

But it your case be such as is spoken of in the doctrine, it is surely time for you to seek a better hope, and another work of God's Spirit, than ever you have yet experienced; something more thorough and effectual. When you see and find by experience, that the seed which was sown in your hearts, though at first it sprang up and seemed flourishing, yet is withering away, as by the heat of the sun, or is choked, as with thorns; this shows in what sort of ground the seed was sown, that it is either stony or thorny ground; and that therefore it is necessary you should pass through another change, whereby your heart may become good ground, which shall bring forth fruit with patience.

I insist not on that as a reason why you should not throw away your hope, that you had the judgment of others, that the change of which you were the subject was right. It is a small matter to be judged of man's judgment, whether you be approved or condemned, and whether it be by minister or people, wise or unwise. 1 Cor. 4:3. "It is a very small thing that I should be judged of you or of man's judgment." If your goodness have proved to be as the morning cloud and early dew, if you be one of those who have forsaken God and left off calling upon his name, you have the judgment of God, and the sentence of God in the Scriptures against you, which is a thousand times more than to have the judgment of all the wise and godly men and ministers in the world in your favor.

Others, from your account of things, may have been obliged to have charity for you, and to think that, provided you were not mistaken, and in your account did not misrepresent things, or express them by wrong terms, you were really converted. But what a miserable foundation is this, upon which to build an hope as to your eternal state!

Here I request your attention to a few things in particular, which I have to say to you concerning your hope.

1. *Why will you retain that hope which by evident experience you find poisons you?* Is it reasonable to think, that a holy hope, a hope that is from heaven,

would have such an influence? No, surely; nothing of such a malignant influence comes from that world of purity and glory. No poison groweth in the paradise of God. The same hope which leads men to sin in this world will lead to Hell hereafter. Why therefore will you retain such an hope, of which your own experience shows you the ill tendency, in that it encourages you to lead a wicked life? For certainly that life is a wicked life wherein you live in the neglect of so well known a duty as that of secret prayer, and in the disobedience of so plain a command of God, as that by which this duty is enjoined. And is not a way of disobedience to God a way to Hell?

If your own experience of the nature and tendency of your hope will not convince you of the falseness of it, what will? Are you resolved to retain your hope, let it prove ever so unsound and hurtful? Will you hold it fast till you go to Hell with it? Many men cling to a false hope, and embrace it so closely, that they never let it go till the flames of Hell cause their arms to unclench and let go their hold. Consider how you will answer it at the day of judgment when God shall call you to an account for your folly in resting in such an hope. Will it be a sufficient answer for you to say, that you had the charity of others, and that they thought your conversion was right?

Certainly it is foolish for men to imagine, that God had no more wisdom, or could contrive no other way of bestowing comfort and hope of eternal life than one which should encourage men to forsake him.

2. How is your conduct consistent with loving God above all? If you have not a spirit to love God above your dearest earthly friends, and your most pleasant earthly enjoyments; the scriptures are very plain, and full in it, that you are not true Christians. But if you had indeed such a spirit, would you thus grow weary of the practice of drawing near to him, and become habitually so averse to it, as in a great measure to cast off so plain a duty which is so much the life of a child of God? It is the nature of love to be averse to absence, and to love a near access to those whom we love. We love to be with them; we delight to come often to them, and to have much conversation with them. But when a person who hath heretofore been wont to converse freely with another, by degrees forsakes him, grows strange, and converses with him but little, and that although the other be importunate with him for the continuance of their former intimacy; this plainly shows the coldness of his heart towards him.

The neglect of the duty of prayer seems to be inconsistent with supreme love to God also upon another account, and that is, that it is against the will of God so plainly revealed. True love to God seeks to please God in everything, and universally to conform to his will.

3. Your thus restraining prayer before God is not only inconsistent with the love—but also with the fear—of God. It is an argument that you cast off fear, as is manifest by that text, Job 15:4. "Yea, thou castest off fear, and restrainest prayer before God." While you thus live in the transgression of so plain a command of God, you evidently show, that there is no fear of God before your eyes. Psal. 36:1: "The transgression of the wicked saith within my heart, that there is no fear of God before his eyes."

4. Consider how living in such a neglect is inconsistent with leading a holy life. We are abundantly instructed in scripture, that true Christians do lead a holy life; that without holiness no man shall see the Lord, Heb. 12:14; and that every one that hath this hope in him, purifieth himself, even as Christ is pure, 1 John 3:3. In Prov.16:17, it is said, "The highway of the upright is to depart from evil," i.e. it is, as it were, the common beaten road in which all the godly travel. To the like purpose is Isa. 35:8. "A highway shall be there, and a way, and it shall be called the way of holiness; the unclean shall not pass over it, but it shall be for those," i.e. those redeemed persons spoken of in the foregoing verses. It is spoken of in Rom. 8:1, as the character of all believers, that they walk not after the flesh, but after the spirit.

But how is a life, in a great measure prayerless, consistent with a holy life? To lead a holy life is to lead a life devoted to God; a life of worshiping and serving God; a life consecrated to the service of God. But how doth he lead such a life who doth not so much as maintain the duty of prayer? How can such a man be said to walk by the Spirit and to be a servant of the Most High God? A holy life is a life of faith. The life that true Christians live in the world, they live by the faith of the Son of God. But who can believe that man lives by faith, who lives without prayer, which is the natural expression of faith? Prayer is as natural an expression of faith as breathing is of life; and to say a man lives a life of faith, and yet lives a prayerless life, is every whit as inconsistent and incredible, as to say, that a man lives without breathing. A prayerless life is so far from being a holy life, that it is a profane life. He that lives so, lives like an heathen, who calleth not on God's name; he that lives a prayerless life, lives without God in the world.

5. If you live in the neglect of secret prayer, you show your good will to neglect all the worship of God. He that prays only when he prays with others, would not pray at all, were it not that the eyes of others are upon him. He that will not pray where none but God seeth him, manifestly doth not pray at all out of respect to God, or regard to his all-seeing eye, and therefore doth in effect cast off all prayer. And he that casts off prayer, in effect casts off all the worship of God, of which prayer is the principal duty. Now, what a miserable saint is he who is no worshiper of God! He that casts off the worship of God, in effect casts off God himself: he refuses to own him, or to be conversant with him as his God. For the way in which men own God, and are conversant with him as their God, is by worshiping him.

6. *How can you expect to dwell with God for ever, if you so neglect and forsake him here?* This your practice shows, that you place not your happiness in God, in nearness to him, and communion with him. He who refuses to come and visit, and converse with a friend, and who in a great measure forsakes him, when he is abundantly invited and importuned to come; plainly shows that he places not his happiness in the company and conversation of that friend. Now, if this be the case with you respecting God, then how can you expect to have it for your happiness to all eternity, to be with God, and to enjoy holy communion with him?

Let those persons who hope they are converted, and yet have in a great measure left off the duty of secret prayer, and whose manner it is ordinarily to neglect it, for their own sake seriously consider these things. For what will profit then to please themselves with that, while they live, which will fail them at last, and leave them in fearful and amazing disappointment?

It is probable, that some of you who have entertained a good opinion of your state, and have looked upon yourselves as converts; but have of late in a great measure left off the duty of secret prayer; will this evening attend secret prayer, and so continue to do for a little while; after your hearing this sermon, to the end, that you may solve the difficulty, and the objection which is made against the truth of your hope. But this will not hold. As it hath been in former instances of the like nature, so what you now hear will have such effect upon you but a little while. When the business and cares of the world shall again begin to crowd a little upon you, or next time you shall go out into young company, it is probable you will again neglect this duty. The next time a frolic shall be appointed, to which it is proposed to you to go, it is highly probable you will neglect not only secret prayer; but also family prayer. Or at least, after a while, you will come to the same pass again, as before, in casting off fear and restraining prayer before God.

It is not very likely that you will ever be constant and persevering in this duty, until you shall have obtained a better principle in your hearts. The streams which have no springs to feed them will dry up. The drought and heat consume the snow waters. Although they run plentifully in the spring, yet when the sun ascends higher with a burning heat they are gone.

The seed that is sown in stony places, though it seem to flourish at present, yet as the sun shall rise with a burning heat, will wither away. None will bring forth fruit with patience, but those whose hearts are become good ground.

Without any heavenly seed remaining in them, men may whenever they fall in among the godly, continue all their lives to talk like saints. They may, for their credit's sake, tell of what they have experienced But their deeds will not hold. They may continue to tell of their inward experiences, and yet live in the neglect of secret prayer, and of other duties.

II. I would take occasion from this doctrine to exhort all to persevere in the duty of prayer.

This exhortation is much insisted on in the word of God. It is insisted on in the Old Testament; 1 Chron. 16:11: "Seek the Lord and his strength, seek his face continually." Isai. 62:7. "Ye that make mention of the Lord, keep not silence;" i.e. be not silent as to the voice of prayer, as is manifest by the following words, "and give him no rest till he establish and till he make Jerusalem a praise in the earth," Israel of old is reproved for growing weary of the duty of prayer. Isai. 43:22. "But thou hast not called upon me, O Jacob, but thou hast been weary of me, O Israel."

Perseverance in the duty of prayer is very much insisted on in the New Testament; as Luke 18 at the beginning, "A man ought always to pray, and not to faint;" i.e. not to be discouraged or weary of the duty; but should always continue in it. Again, Luke 21:36. "Watch ye therefore, and pray always." We have the example of Anna the prophetess set before us, Luke 1:36, etc., who, though she had lived to be more than an hundred years old, yet never was weary of this duty. It is said, "She departed not from the temple, but served God, with fastings and prayers, night and day." Cornelius also is commended for his constancy in this duty. It is said, that he prayed to God always; Acts 10:2. The Apostle Paul, in his epistles, insists very much on constancy in this duty; Rom. 12:12. "Continuing instant in prayer." Eph. 6:18,19. "Praying always with all prayer and supplication in the Spirit, and watching thereunto with all perseverance." Col. 4:2. "Continue in prayer, and watch in the same." 1 Thess. 5:17. "Pray without ceasing." To the same effect the Apostle Peter, 1 Pet. 4:7. "Watch unto prayer."

Thus abundantly the scripture insists upon it, that we should persevere in the duty of prayer; which shows that, it is of very great importance that we should persevere. If the contrary be the manner of hypocrites, as hath been shown in the doctrine, then surely we ought to beware of this leaven.

But here let the following things be particularly considered as motives to perseverance in this duty.

1. *That perseverance in the way of duty is necessary to salvation, and is abundantly declared so to be in the holy scriptures;* as Isai. 64:5:

> Thou meetest him that rejoiceth and worketh righteousness, those that remember thee in thy ways: Behold, thou art wroth, for we have sinned: In those is continuance, and we shall be saved.

Heb. 10:38, 39:

> Now the just shall live by faith: But if any man draw back, my soul hath no pleasure in him. But we are not of them who draw back unto perdition; but of them that believe to the saving of the soul.

Rom. 11:22:

> Behold therefore the goodness and severity of God: On them which fell, severity; but towards thee, goodness, if thou continue in his goodness; otherwise thou also shalt be cut off. . .

So in many other places.

Many, when they think they are converted, seem to imagine that their work is done, and that there is nothing else needful in order to their going to heaven. Indeed perseverance in holiness of life is not necessary to salvation, as the righteousness by which a right to salvation is obtained. Nor is actual perseverance necessary in order to our becoming interested in that righteousness by which we are justified. For as soon as ever a soul hath believed in Christ, or hath put forth one act of faith in him, it becomes interested in his righteousness, and in all the promises purchased by it.

But persevering in the way of duty is necessary to salvation, as a concomitant and evidence of a title to salvation. There is never a title to salvation without it, though it be not the righteousness by which a title to salvation is obtained. It is necessary to salvation, as it is the necessary consequence of true faith. It is an evidence which universally attends uprightness, and the defect of it is an infallible evidence of the want of uprightness. Psal. 125:4, 5 [says that] there, such as are good and upright in heart are distinguished from such as fall away or turn aside:

> Do good, O Lord, to those that are good, and to them that are upright in their hearts. As for such as turn aside to their crooked ways, the Lord shall lead them forth with the workers of iniquity. But peace shall be upon Israel.

It is mentioned as an evidence that the hearts of the children of Israel were not right with God, that they did not persevere in the ways of holiness. Psal. 78:8. "A generation that set not their heart[s] aright, and whose spirit was not steadfast with God."

Christ gives this as a distinguishing character of those that are his disciples indeed, and of a true and saving faith, that it is accompanied with perseverance in the obedience of Christ's word. John 8:31: "Then said Jesus to those Jews which believed on him, if ye continue in my word, then are ye my disciples indeed." This is mentioned as a necessary evidence of an interest in Christ, Heb. 3:14. "We are made partakers of Christ, if we hold the beginning of our confidence steadfast to the end."

Perseverance is not only a necessary concomitant and evidence of a title to salvation; but also a necessary prerequisite to the actual possession of eternal life. It is the only way to heaven, the narrow way that leadeth to life. Hence Christ exhorts the church of Philadelphia to persevere in holiness from this consideration, that it was necessary in order to her obtaining the crown.

> Hold fast that which thou hast, that no man take thy crown. (Rev. 3:11.)

It is necessary, not only that persons should once have been walking in the way of duty, but that they should be found so doing when Christ cometh.

> Blessed is that servant whom his lord, when he cometh, shall find so doing. (Luke 9:43.)

Holding out to the end is often made the condition of actual salvation.

> He that endureth to the end, the same shall be saved. (Mat. 10:22.)

> Be thou faithful unto death, and I will give thee a crown of life. (Rev. 2:10.)

2. In order to your own perseverance in the way of duty, your own care and watchfulness are necessary. For though it be promised that true saints shall persevere, yet that is no argument that their care and watchfulness is not necessary in order to it; because their care to keep the commands of God is the thing promised. If the saints should fail of care, watchfulness, and diligence to persevere in holiness, that failure of their care and diligence would itself be a failure of holiness. They who persevere not in watchfulness and diligence, persevere not in holiness of life, for holiness of life very much consists in watchfulness and diligence to keep the commands of God. It is one promise of the covenant of grace, that the Saints shall keep God's commandments. (Ezek. 9:19, 20.) Yet that is no argument that they have no need to take care to keep these commandments, or to do their duty. So the promise of God, that the saints shall persevere in holiness, is no argument that it is not necessary that they should take heed lest they fall away.

Therefore the scriptures abundantly warn men to watch over themselves diligently, and to give earnest heed lest they fall away.

> Watch ye, stand fast in the faith, quit you like men, be strong. (1 Cor. 15:13.)

> Let him that thinketh he standeth, take heed lest he fall. (1 Cor. 10:12.)

> Take heed, brethren, lest there be in any of you an evil heart of unbelief in departing from the living God; but exhort one another daily, while it is called to-day, lest any of you be hardened through the deceitfulness of sin. For we are made partakers of Christ, if we hold the beginning of our confidence steadfast unto the end. (Heb. 3:12, 13, 14.)

> Let us therefore fear, lest a promise being left us of entering into his rest, any of you should seem to come short of it. (Heb. 4:1.)

> Ye therefore, beloved, seeing ye know these things before, beware lest ye also, being led away with the error of the wicked, fall from your own steadfastness. (2 Peter 3:17.)

> Look to yourselves that we lose not those things which we have wrought, but that we receive a full reward. (2 John 5:8.)

Thus you see how earnestly the scriptures press on Christians exhortations to take diligent heed to themselves that they fall not away. And certainly these cautions are not without reason.

The scriptures particularly insist upon watchfulness in order to perseverance in the duty of prayer. Watch and pray, saith Christ; which implies that we should watch unto prayer, as the Apostle Peter says, 1 Pet. 4:7. It implies that we should watch against a neglect of prayer, as well as against other sins. The apostle, in places which have been already mentioned, directs us to pray with all prayer, watching there unto with all perseverance, and to continue in prayer, and watch in the same. Nor is it any wonder that the apostles so much insisted on watching, in order to a continuance in prayer with all perseverance; for there are many temptations to neglect this duty; first to be inconstant in it, and from time to time to omit it; then in a great measure to neglect it. The devil watches to draw us away from God, and to hinder us from going to him in prayer. We are surrounded with one and another tempting object, business, and diversion: particularly we meet with many things which are great temptations to a neglect of this duty.

3. To move you to persevere in the duty of prayer, consider how much you always stand in need of the help of God. If persons who have formerly attended this duty, leave it off, the language of it is, that now they stand in no further need of God's help, that they have no further occasion to go to God with requests and supplications: when indeed it is in God we live, and move, and have our being. We cannot draw a breath without his help. You need his help every day, for the supply of your outward wants; and especially you stand in continual need of him to help your souls. Without his protection they would immediately fall into the hands of the devil, who always stands as a roaring lion, ready, whenever he is permitted, to fall upon the souls of men and devour them. If God should indeed preserve your lives, but should otherwise forsake and leave you to yourselves, you would be most miserable: your lives would be a curse to you.

Those that are converted, if God should forsake them, would soon fall away totally from a state of grace into a state more miserable than ever they were in before their conversion. They have no strength of their own to resist those powerful enemies who surround them. Sin and Satan would immediately carry them away, as a mighty flood, if God should forsake them. You stand in need of daily supplies from God. Without God you can receive no spiritual light nor comfort, can exercise no grace, can bring forth no fruit. Without God your souls will wither and pine away, and sink into a most wretched state. You continually need the instructions and directions of God. What can a little child do, in a vast howling wilderness, without some one to guide it, and to lead it in the right way? Without God you will soon fall into snares, and pits, and many fatal calamities.

Seeing therefore you stand in such continual need of the help of God, how reasonable is it that you should continually seek it of him, and perseveringly acknowledge your dependence upon him, by resorting to him, to spread your needs before him, and to offer up your requests to him in prayer. Let us consider how miserable we should be, if we should leave off prayer, and God at the same time should leave off to take any care of us, or to afford us any more supplies of his grace. By our constancy in prayer, we cannot be profitable to God; and if we leave it off, God will sustain no damage: he doth not need our prayers; Job 10:6, 7. But if God cease to care for us and to help us, we immediately sink: we can do nothing: we can receive nothing without him.

4. Consider the great benefit of a constant, diligent, and persevering attendance on this duty. It is one of the greatest and most excellent means of nourishing the new nature, and of causing the soul to flourish and prosper. It is an excellent means of keeping up an acquaintance with God, and of growing in the knowledge of God. It is the way to a life of communion with God. It is an excellent means of taking off the heart from the vanities of the world and of causing the mind to be conversant in heaven. It is an excellent preservative from sin and the wiles of the devil, and a powerful antidote against the poison of the old serpent. It is a duty whereby strength is derived from God against the lusts and corruptions of the heart, and the snares of the world.

It hath a great tendency to keep the soul in a wakeful frame, and to lead us to a strict walk with God, and to a life that shall be fruitful in such good works, as tend to adorn the doctrine of Christ, and to cause our light so to shine before others, that they, seeing our good works, shall glorify our Father who is in heaven And if the duty be constantly and diligently attended, it will be a very pleasant duty. Slack and slothful attendance upon it, and unsteadiness in it, are the causes which make it so great a burden as it is to some persons. Their slothfulness in it hath naturally the effect to beget a dislike of the duty and a great indisposition to it. But if it be constantly and diligently attended, it is one of the best means of leading not only a Christian and amiable, but also a pleasant life; a life of much sweet fellowship with Christ, and of the abundant enjoyment of the light of his countenance.

Besides, the great power which prayer, when duly attended, hath with God, is worthy of your notice. By it men become like Jacob, who, as a prince, had power with God, and prevailed, when he wrestled with God for the blessing. See the power of prayer represented in James 5:16,18. By these things you may be sensible how much you will lose, if you shall be negligent of this great duty of calling upon God; and how ill you will consult your own interest by such a neglect.

Conclusion

I. I conclude my discourse with two directions in order to constancy and perseverance in this duty.

1. Watch against the beginnings of a neglect of this duty. Persons who have for a time practiced this duty, and afterwards neglect it, commonly leave it off by degrees. While their convictions and religious affections last, they are very constant in their closets, and no worldly business, or company, or diversion hinders them. But as their convictions and affections begin to die away, they begin to find excuses to neglect it sometimes. They are now so hurried; they have now such and such things to attend to; or there are now such inconveniences in the way, that they persuade themselves they may very excusably omit it for this time. Afterwards it pretty frequently so happens, that they have something to hinder, something which they call a just excuse. After a while, a less thing becomes a sufficient excuse than was allowed to be such at first. Thus the person by degrees contracts more and more of an habit of neglecting prayer, and becomes more and more indisposed to it. And even when he doth perform it, it is in such a poor, dull, heartless, miserable manner, that he says to himself, he might as well not do it at all, as do it so. Thus he makes his own dullness and indisposition an excuse for wholly neglecting it, or at least for living in a great measure in the neglect of it. After this manner do Satan and men's own corruptions inveigle them to their ruin.

Therefore beware of the first beginnings of a neglect. Watch against temptations to it: take heed how you begin to allow of excuses. Be watchful to keep up the duty in the height of it; let it not so much as begin to sink. For when you give way, though it be but little, it is like giving way to an enemy in the field of battle; the first beginning of a retreat greatly encourages the enemy, and weakens the retreating soldiers.

2. *Let me direct you to forsake all such practices as you find by experience do indispose you to the duty of secret prayer.* Examine the things in which you have allowed yourselves, and inquire whether they have had this effect. You are able to look over your past behavior, and may doubtless, on an impartial consideration, make a judgment of the practices and courses in which you have allowed yourselves.

Particularly let young people examine their manner of company keeping, and the round of diversions in which, with their companions, they have allowed themselves. I only desire that you would ask at the mouth of your own consciences what has been the effect of these things with respect to your attendance on the duty of secret prayer. Have you not found that such practices have tended to the neglect of this duty? Have you not found that after them you have been more indisposed to it, and less conscientious and careful to attend it? Yea have they not from, time to time, actually been the means of your neglecting it?

If you cannot deny that this is really the case, then, if you seek the good of your souls, forsake these practices. Whatever you may plead for them, as that there is no hurt in them, or that there is a time for all things, and the like; yet if you find this hurt in the consequence of them, it is time for you to forsake them. And if you value heaven more than a little worldly diversion; if you set an higher price on eternal glory than on a dance or a song, you will forsake them.

If these things be lawful in themselves, yet if your experience show, that they are attended with such a consequence as I have now mentioned, that is enough. It is lawful in itself for you to enjoy your right hand and your right eye. But if, by experience, you find they cause you to offend, it is time for you to cut off the one, and pluck out the other, as you would rather go to heaven without them than go to Hell with them, into that place of torment where the worm dieth not, and the fire is not quenched.

Sinners in the Hands of an Angry God

Edwards, on a missionary tour at Enfield, Connecticut on July 8, 1741, preached this sermon to try to wake his complacent hearers from their spiritual torpor. By far the most famous of Edwards' writing, its original delivery "caused an immediate and general revival of religion throughout the place." (*Memoirs of Jonathan Edwards*.)

"Their foot shall slide in due time."—*Deuteronomy 32:35*

In this verse is threatened the vengeance of God on the wicked unbelieving Israelites, who were God's visible people, and who lived under the means of grace; but who, notwithstanding all God's wonderful works towards them, remained (as vers 28.) void of counsel, having no understanding in them. Under all the cultivations of heaven, they brought forth bitter and poisonous fruit; as in the two verses next preceding the text.

The expression I have chosen for my text, "their foot shall slide in due time," seems to imply the following things, relating to the punishment and destruction to which these wicked Israelites were exposed.

- *That they were always exposed to destruction; as one that stands or walks in slippery places is always exposed to fall.* This is implied in the manner of their destruction coming upon them, being represented by their foot sliding. The same is expressed in Psalm 72:18: "Surely thou didst set them in slippery places; thou castedst them down into destruction."

- *It implies, that they were always exposed to sudden unexpected destruction.* As he that walks in slippery places is every moment liable to fall, he cannot foresee one moment whether he shall stand or fall the next; and when he does fall, he falls at once without warning, which is also expressed in Psalm 73:18,19. "Surely thou didst set them in slippery places; thou castedst them down into destruction: How are they brought into desolation as in a moment!"

- *Another thing implied is, that they are liable to fall of themselves*, without being thrown down by the hand of another; as he that stands or walks on slippery ground needs nothing but his own weight to throw him down.

- *That the reason why they are not fallen already and do not fall now is only that God's appointed time is not come.* For it is said, that when that due time, or appointed time comes, *"their foot shall slide."* Then they shall be left to fall, as they are inclined by their own weight. God will not hold them up in these slippery places any longer, but will let them go; and then, at that very instant, they shall fall into destruction; as he that stands on such slippery declining ground, on the edge of a pit, he cannot stand alone, when he is let go he immediately falls and is lost.

Doctrine

The observation from the words that I would now insist upon is this. *"There is nothing that keeps wicked men at any one moment out of Hell, but the mere pleasure of God."* By the *mere* pleasure of God, I mean his *sovereign* pleasure, his arbitrary will, restrained by no obligation, hindered by no manner of difficulty, any more than if nothing else but God's mere will had in the least degree, or in any respect whatsoever, any hand in the preservation of wicked men one moment. The truth of this observation may appear by the following considerations.

1. There is no want of power in God to cast wicked men into Hell at any moment. Men's hands cannot be strong when God rises up. The strongest have no power to resist him, nor can any deliver out of his hands. He is not only able to cast wicked men into Hell, but he can most easily do it. Sometimes an earthly prince meets with a great deal of difficulty to subdue a rebel, who has found means to fortify himself, and has made himself strong by the numbers of his followers. But it is not so with God. There is no fortress that is any defense from the power of God. Though hand join in hand, and vast multitudes of God's enemies combine and associate themselves, they are easily broken in pieces. They are as great heaps of light chaff before the whirlwind; or large quantities of dry stubble before devouring flames. We find it easy to tread on and crush a worm that we see crawling on the earth; so it is easy for us to cut or singe a slender thread that anything hangs by: thus easy is it for God, when he pleases, to cast his enemies down to Hell. What are we, that we should think to stand before him, at whose rebuke the earth trembles, and before whom the rocks are thrown down?

2. *They deserve to be cast into Hell; so that divine justice never stands in the way, it makes no objection against God's using his power at any moment to destroy them.* Yea, on the contrary, justice calls aloud for an infinite punishment of their sins. Divine justice says of the tree that brings forth such grapes of Sodom, "Cut it down, why cumbereth it the ground?" Luke 13:7. The sword of divine justice is every moment brandished over their heads, and it is nothing but the hand of arbitrary mercy, and God's mere will, that holds it back.

3. *They are already under a sentence of condemnation to Hell.* They do not only justly deserve to be cast down thither, but the sentence of the law of God, that eternal and immutable rule of righteousness that God has fixed between him and mankind, is gone out against them, and stands against them; so that they are bound over already to Hell. John 3:18. "He that believeth not is condemned already." So that every unconverted man properly belongs to Hell; that is his place; from thence he is, John 8:23. "Ye are from beneath:" And thither he is bound; it is the place that justice, and God's word, and the sentence of his unchangeable law assign to him.

4. *They are now the objects of that very same anger and wrath of God, that is expressed in the torments of Hell.* And the reason why they do not go down to Hell at each moment, is not because God, in whose power they are, is not then very angry with them; as he is with many miserable creatures now tormented in Hell, who there feel and bear the fierceness of his wrath. Yea, God is a great deal more angry with great numbers that are now on earth: yea, doubtless, with many that are now in this congregation, who it may be are at ease, than he is with many of those who are now in the flames of Hell.

So that it is not because God is unmindful of their wickedness, and does not resent it, that he does not let loose his hand and cut them off. God is not altogether such an one as themselves, though they may imagine him to be so. The wrath of God burns against them, their damnation does not slumber; the pit is prepared, the fire is made ready, the furnace is now hot, ready to receive them; the flames do now rage and glow. The glittering sword is whet, and held over them, and the pit hath opened its mouth under them.

5. *The devil stands ready to fall upon them, and seize them as his own, at what moment God shall permit him.* They belong to him; he has their souls in his possession, and under his dominion. The scripture represents them as his goods, Luke 11:12. The devils watch them; they are ever by them at their right hand; they stand waiting for them, like greedy hungry lions that see their prey, and expect to have it, but are for the present kept back. If God should withdraw his hand, by which they are restrained, they would in one moment fly upon their poor souls. The old serpent is gaping for them; Hell opens its mouth wide to receive them; and if God should permit it, they would be hastily swallowed up and lost.

6. *There are in the souls of wicked men those hellish principles reigning, that would presently kindle and flame out into Hell fire, if it were not for God's restraints.* There is laid in the very nature of carnal men, a foundation for the torments of Hell. There are those corrupt principles, in reigning power in them, and in full possession of them, that are seeds of Hell fire. These principles are active and powerful, exceeding violent in their nature, and if it were not for the restraining hand of God upon them, they would soon break out, they would flame out after the same manner as the same corruptions, the same enmity does in the hearts of damned souls, and would beget the same torments as they do in them. The souls of the wicked are in scripture compared to the troubled sea, Isa. 57:20. For the present, God restrains their wickedness by his mighty power, as he does the raging waves of the troubled sea, saying, "Hitherto shalt thou come, but no further;" but if God should withdraw that restraining power, it would soon carry all before it. Sin is the ruin and misery of the soul; it is destructive in its nature; and if God should leave it without restraint, there would need nothing else to make the soul perfectly miserable. The corruption of the heart of man is immoderate and boundless in its fury; and while wicked men live here, it is like fire pent up by God's restraints, whereas if it were let loose, it would set on fire the course of nature; and as the heart is now a sink of sin, so if sin was not restrained, it would immediately turn the soul into a fiery oven, or a furnace of fire and brimstone.

7. *It is no security to wicked men for one moment, that there are no visible means of death at hand.* It is no security to a natural man, that he is now in health, and that he does not see which way he should now immediately go out of the world by any accident, and that there is no visible danger in any

respect in his circumstances. The manifold and continual experience of the world in all ages, shows this is no evidence that a man is not on the very brink of eternity, and that the next step will not be into another world. The unseen, unthought-of ways and means of persons going suddenly out of the world are innumerable and inconceivable. Unconverted men walk over the pit of Hell on a rotten covering, and there are innumerable places in this covering so weak that it will not bear their weight, and these places are not seen. The arrows of death fly unseen at noon-day; the sharpest sight cannot discern them. God has so many different unsearchable ways of taking wicked men out of the world and sending them to Hell, that there is nothing to make it appear that God had need to be at the expense of a miracle, or go out of the ordinary course of his providence, to destroy any wicked man, at any moment. All the means that there are of sinners going out of the world, are so in God's hands, and so universally and absolutely subject to his power and determination, that it does not depend at all the less on the mere will of God, whether sinners shall at any moment go to Hell, than if means were never made use of, or at all concerned in the case.

Natural men's prudence and care to preserve their own lives, or the care of others to preserve them, do not secure them a moment. To this, divine providence and universal experience do also bear testimony. There is this clear evidence that men's own wisdom is no security to them from death; that if it were otherwise we should see some difference between the wise and politic men of the world, and others, with regard to their liableness to early and unexpected death: but how is it in fact? Eccles. 2:16: "How dieth the wise man? Even as the fool."

8. *All wicked men's pains and contrivance which they use to escape Hell, while they continue to reject Christ, and so remain wicked men, do not secure them from Hell one moment.* Almost every natural man that hears of Hell, flatters himself that he shall escape it; he depends upon himself for his own security; he flatters himself in what he has done, in what he is now doing, or what he intends to do. Every one lays out matters in his own mind how he shall avoid damnation, and flatters himself that he contrives well for himself, and that his schemes will not fail. They hear indeed that there are but few saved, and that the greater part of men that have died heretofore are gone to Hell; but each one imagines that he lays out matters better for his own escape than others have done. He does not intend to come to that place of torment; he says within himself, that he intends to take effectual care, and to order matters so for himself as not to fail.

But the foolish children of men miserably delude themselves in their own schemes, and in confidence in their own strength and wisdom; they trust to nothing but a shadow. The greater part of those who heretofore have lived under the same means of grace, and are now dead, are undoubtedly gone to Hell; and it was not because they were not as wise as those who are now alive: it was not because they did not lay out matters as well for themselves to secure their own escape. If we could speak with them, and inquire of them, one by one, whether they expected, when alive, and when they used to hear about Hell, ever to be the subjects of misery: we doubtless, should hear one and another reply,

> No, I never intended to come here: I had laid out matters otherwise in my mind; I thought I should contrive well for myself. I thought my scheme good. I intended to take effectual care; but it came upon me unexpected; I did not look for it at that time, and in that manner; it came as a thief. Death outwitted me: God's wrath was too quick for me. Oh, my cursed foolishness! I was flattering myself, and pleasing myself with vain dreams of what I would do hereafter; and when I was saying, Peace and safety, then sudden destruction came upon me.

9. God has laid himself under no obligation, by any promise, to keep any natural man out of Hell one moment. God certainly has made no promises either of eternal life, or of any deliverance or preservation from eternal death, but what are contained in the covenant of grace, the promises that are given in Christ, in whom all the promises are yea and amen. But surely they have no interest in the promises of the covenant of grace who are not the children of the covenant, who do not believe in any of the promises, and have no interest in the Mediator of the covenant.

So that, whatever some have imagined and pretended about promises made to natural men's earnest seeking and knocking, it is plain and manifest, that whatever pains a natural man takes in religion, whatever prayers he makes, till he believes in Christ, God is under no manner of obligation to keep him a moment from eternal destruction.

So that, thus it is that natural men are held in the hand of God, over the pit of Hell; they have deserved the fiery pit, and are already sentenced to it; and God is dreadfully provoked, his anger is as great towards them as to those that are actually suffering the executions of the fierceness of his wrath in Hell, and they have done nothing in the least to appease or abate that anger, neither is God in the least bound by any promise to hold them up one moment; the devil is waiting for them, Hell is gaping for them, the flames gather and flash about them, and would fain lay hold on them, and swallow them up; the fire pent up in their own hearts is struggling to break out: and they have no interest in any Mediator, there are no means within reach that can be any security to them. In short, they have no refuge, nothing to take hold of; all that preserves them every moment is the mere arbitrary will, and uncovenanted, unobliged forbearance of an incensed God.

Application

The use of this awful subject may be for awakening unconverted persons in this congregation. This that you have heard is the case of every one of you that are out of Christ. That world of misery, that lake of burning brimstone, is extended abroad under you. There is the dreadful pit of the glowing flames of the wrath of God; there is Hell's wide gaping mouth open; and you have nothing to stand upon, nor anything to take hold of; there is nothing between you and Hell but the air; it is only the power and mere pleasure of God that holds you up.

You probably are not sensible of this; you find you are kept out of Hell, but do not see the hand of God in it; but look at other things, as the good state of your bodily constitution, your care of your own life, and the means you use for your own preservation. But indeed these things are nothing; if God should withdraw his hand, they would avail no more to keep you from falling, than the thin air to hold up a person that is suspended in it.

Your wickedness makes you as it were heavy as lead, and to tend downwards with great weight and pressure towards Hell; and if God should let you go, you would immediately sink and swiftly descend and plunge into the bottomless gulf, and your healthy constitution, and your own care and prudence, and best contrivance, and all your righteousness, would have no more influence to uphold you and keep you out of Hell, than a spider's web would have to stop a falling rock. Were it not for the sovereign pleasure of God, the earth would not bear you one moment; for you are a burden to it; the creation groans with you; the creature is made subject to the bondage of your corruption, not willingly; the sun does not willingly shine upon you to give you light to serve sin and Satan; the earth does not willingly yield her increase to satisfy your lusts; nor is it willingly a stage for your wickedness to be acted upon; the air does not willingly serve you for breath to maintain the flame of life in your vitals, while you spend your life in the service of God's enemies. God's creatures are good, and were made for men to serve God with, and do not willingly subserve to any

other purpose, and groan when they are abused to purposes so directly contrary to their nature and end. And the world would spew you out, were it
not for the sovereign hand of him who hath subjected it in hope. There are
the black clouds of God's wrath now hanging directly over your heads, full
of the dreadful storm, and big with thunder; and were it not for the restraining hand of God, it would immediately burst forth upon you. The sovereign pleasure of God, for the present, stays his rough wind; otherwise it
would come with fury, and your destruction would come like a whirlwind,
and you would be like the chaff on the summer threshing floor.

The wrath of God is like great waters that are dammed for the present;
they increase more and more, and rise higher and higher, till an outlet is
given; and the longer the stream is stopped, the more rapid and mighty is its
course, when once it is let loose. It is true that judgment against your evil
works has not been executed hitherto; the floods of God's vengeance have
been withheld; but your guilt in the meantime is constantly increasing, and
you are every day treasuring up more wrath; the waters are constantly rising, and waxing more and more mighty; and there is nothing but the mere
pleasure of God, that holds the waters back, that are unwilling to be
stopped, and press hard to go forward. If God should only withdraw his
hand from the flood-gate, it would immediately fly open, and the fiery
floods of the fierceness and wrath of God, would rush forth with inconceivable fury, and would come upon you with omnipotent power; and if your
strength were ten thousand times greater than it is, yea, ten thousand times
greater than the strength of the stoutest, sturdiest devil in Hell, it would be
nothing to withstand or endure it.

The bow of God's wrath is bent, and the arrow made ready on the
string, and justice bends the arrow at your heart, and strains the bow, and it
is nothing but the mere pleasure of God, and that of an angry God, without
any promise or obligation at all, that keeps the arrow one moment from being made drunk with your blood. Thus all you that never passed under a
great change of heart, by the mighty power of the Spirit of God upon your
souls; all you that were never born again, and made new creatures, and
raised from being dead in sin, to a state of new, and before altogether
unexperienced light and life, are in the hands of an angry God. However
you may have reformed your life in many things, and may have had religious affections, and may keep up a form of religion in your families and
closets, and in the house of God, it is nothing but his mere pleasure that
keeps you from being this moment swallowed up in everlasting destruction. However unconvinced you may now be of the truth of what you hear,

by and by you will be fully convinced of it. Those that are gone from being in the like circumstances with you, see that it was so with them; for destruction came suddenly upon most of them; when they expected nothing of it, and while they were saying, "Peace and safety." Now they see that those things on which they depended for peace and safety were nothing but thin air and empty shadows.

The God that holds you over the pit of Hell, much as one holds a spider, or some loathsome insect over the fire, abhors you, and is dreadfully provoked: his wrath towards you burns like fire; he looks upon you as worthy of nothing else, but to be cast into the fire; he is of purer eyes than to bear to have you in his sight; you are ten thousand times more abominable in his eyes, than the most hateful venomous serpent is in ours. You have offended him infinitely more than ever a stubborn rebel did his prince; and yet it is nothing but his hand that holds you from falling into the fire every moment. It is to be ascribed to nothing else, that you did not go to Hell the last night; that you were suffered to awake again in this world, after you closed your eyes to sleep. And there is no other reason to be given, why you have not dropped into Hell since you arose in the morning, but that God's hand has held you up. There is no other reason to be given why you have not gone to Hell, since you have sat here in the house of God, provoking his pure eyes by your sinful wicked manner of attending his solemn worship. Yea, there is nothing else that is to be given as a reason why you do not this very moment drop down into Hell.

O sinner! Consider the fearful danger you are in: it is a great furnace of wrath, a wide and bottomless pit, full of the fire of wrath, that you are held over in the hand of that God, whose wrath is provoked and incensed as much against you, as against many of the damned in Hell. You hang by a slender thread, with the flames of divine wrath flashing about it, and ready every moment to singe it, and burn it asunder; and you have no interest in any Mediator, and nothing to lay hold of to save yourself, nothing to keep off the flames of wrath, nothing of your own, nothing that you ever have done, nothing that you can do, to induce God to spare you one moment.

And consider here more particularly,

1. *Whose wrath it is: it is the wrath of the infinite God.* If it were only the wrath of man, though it were of the most potent prince, it would be comparatively little to be regarded. The wrath of kings is very much dreaded, especially of absolute monarchs, who have the possessions and lives of their subjects wholly in their power, to be disposed of at their mere will.

Prov. 20:2: "The fear of a king is as the roaring of a lion: whoso provoketh him to anger, sinneth against his own soul." The subject that very much enrages an arbitrary prince is liable to suffer the most extreme torments that human art can invent, or human power can inflict. But the greatest earthly potentates in their greatest majesty and strength, and when clothed in their greatest terrors, are but feeble, despicable worms of the dust, in comparison of the great and almighty Creator and King of heaven and earth. It is but little that they can do, when most enraged, and when they have exerted the utmost of their fury. All the kings of the earth, before God, are as grasshoppers; they are nothing, and less than nothing: both their love and their hatred is to be despised. The wrath of the great King of kings, is as much more terrible than theirs, as his majesty is greater. Luke 12:4,5:

> And I say unto you, my friends, "Be not afraid of them that kill the body, and
> after that, have no more that they can do." But I will forewarn you whom you
> shall fear: fear him, which after he hath killed, hath power to cast into Hell:
> yea, I say unto you, "Fear him."

2. It is the fierceness of his wrath that you are exposed to. We often read of the fury of God; as in Isa. 59:18. "According to their deeds, accordingly he will repay fury to his adversaries." So Isa. 66:15: "For behold, the Lord will come with fire, and with his chariots like a whirlwind, to render his anger with fury, and his rebuke with flames of fire." And in many other places. So, in Rev. 19:15, we read of "the wine press of the fierceness and wrath of Almighty God." The words are exceeding terrible. If it had only been said, "the wrath of God," the words would have implied that which is infinitely dreadful: but it is *"the fierceness and wrath of God."* The fury of God! the fierceness of Jehovah! Oh, how dreadful that must be! Who can utter or conceive what such expressions carry in them! But it is also "the fierceness and wrath of *almighty* God." As though there would be a very great manifestation of his almighty power in what the fierceness of his wrath should inflict, as though omnipotence should be as it were enraged, and exerted, as men are wont to exert their strength in the fierceness of their wrath. Oh! then, what will be the consequence! What will become of the poor worms that shall suffer it! Whose hands can be strong? And whose heart can endure? To what a dreadful, inexpressible, inconceivable depth of misery must the poor creature be sunk who shall be the subject of this!

3. Consider this, you that are here present, that yet remain in an unregenerate state—that God will execute the fierceness of his anger, implies that he will inflict wrath without any pity. When God beholds the ineffable extremity of your case, and sees your torment to be so vastly disproportioned to your strength, and sees how your poor soul is crushed, and sinks down, as it were, into an infinite gloom; he will have no compassion upon you, he will not forbear the executions of his wrath, or in the least lighten his hand; there shall be no moderation or mercy, nor will God then at all stay his rough wind; he will have no regard to your welfare, nor be at all careful lest you should suffer too much in any other sense, than only that you shall *not suffer beyond what strict justice requires*. Nothing shall be withheld because it is so hard for you to bear. Ezek. 8:18:

> Therefore will I also deal in fury: mine eye shall not spare, neither will I have pity; and though they cry in mine ears with a loud voice, yet I will not hear them.

Now God stands ready to pity you; this is a day of mercy; you may cry now with some encouragement of obtaining mercy. But when once the day of mercy is past, your most lamentable and dolorous cries and shrieks will be in vain; you will be wholly lost and thrown away of God, as to any regard to your welfare. God will have no other use to put you to, but to suffer misery; you shall be continued in being to no other end; for you will be a vessel of wrath fitted to destruction; and there will be no other use of this vessel, but to be filled full of wrath. God will be so far from pitying you when you cry to him, that it is said he will only "laugh and mock," Prov. 1:25,26, etc.

How awful are those words, Isa. 63:3, which are the words of the great God.

> I will tread them in mine anger, and will trample them in my fury, and their blood shall be sprinkled upon my garments, and I will stain all my raiment.

It is perhaps impossible to conceive of words that carry in them greater manifestations of these three things, viz. contempt, and hatred, and fierceness of indignation. If you cry to God to pity you, he will be so far from pitying you in your doleful case, or showing you the least regard or favor, that instead of that, he will only tread you under foot. And though he will know that you cannot bear the weight of omnipotence treading upon you, yet he will not regard that, but he will crush you under his feet without mercy; he will crush out your blood, and make it fly, and it shall be sprinkled on his garments, so as to stain all his raiment. He will not only hate you, but he will have you in the utmost contempt: no place shall be thought fit for you, but under his feet to be trodden down as the mire of the streets.

4. The misery you are exposed to, is that which God will inflict to that end, that he might show what that wrath of Jehovah is. God hath had it on his heart to show to angels and men, both how excellent his love is, and also how terrible his wrath is. Sometimes earthly kings have a mind to show how terrible their wrath is, by the extreme punishments they would execute on those that would provoke them. Nebuchadnezzar, that mighty and haughty monarch of the Chaldean empire, was willing to show his wrath when enraged with Shadrach, Meshach, and Abednego; and accordingly gave orders that the burning fiery furnace should be heated seven times hotter than it was before; doubtless, it was raised to the utmost degree of fierceness that human art could raise it. But the great God is also willing to show his wrath, and magnify his awful majesty and mighty power in the extreme sufferings of his enemies. Rom. 9:22:

> What if God, willing to show his wrath, and to make his power known, en-
> dured with much long-suffering the vessels of wrath fitted to destruction?

And seeing this is his design, and what he has determined, even to show how terrible the unrestrained wrath, the fury and fierceness of Jehovah is, he will do it to effect. There will be something accomplished and brought to pass that will be dreadful—[and] with a witness. When the great and angry God hath risen up and executed his awful vengeance on the poor sinner, and the wretch is actually suffering the infinite weight and power of his indignation, then will God call upon the whole universe to behold that awful majesty and mighty power that is to be seen in it. Isa. 33:12–14:

> And the people shall be as the burnings of lime, as thorns cut up shall they be
> burnt in the fire. Hear ye that are far off, what I have done; and ye that are
> near, acknowledge my might. The sinners in Zion are afraid; fearfulness hath
> surprised the hypocrites. . .

Thus it will be with you that are in an unconverted state, if you continue in it; the infinite might, and majesty, and terribleness of the omnipotent God shall be magnified upon you, in the ineffable strength of your torments. You shall be tormented in the presence of the holy angels, and in the presence of the Lamb; and when you shall be in this state of suffering, the glorious inhabitants of heaven shall go forth and look on the awful spectacle, that they may see what the wrath and fierceness of the Almighty is; and when they have seen it, they will fall down and adore that great power and majesty. Isa. 66:23,24:

> And it shall come to pass, that from one new moon to another, and from one
> sabbath to another, shall all flesh come to worship before me, saith the Lord.
> And they shall go forth and look upon the carcasses of the men that have

transgressed against me; for their worm shall not die, neither shall their fire be quenched, and they shall be an abhorring unto all flesh.

5. *It is everlasting wrath.* It would be dreadful to suffer this fierceness and wrath of Almighty God one moment; but you must suffer it to all eternity. There will be no end to this exquisite horrible misery. When you look forward, you shall see a long forever, a boundless duration before you, which will swallow up your thoughts, and amaze your soul; and you will absolutely despair of ever having any deliverance, any end, any mitigation, any rest at all. You will know certainly that you must wear out long ages, millions of millions of ages, in wrestling and conflicting with this almighty merciless vengeance; and then when you have so done, when so many ages have actually been spent by you in this manner, you will know that all is but a point to what remains. So that your punishment will indeed be infinite. Oh, who can express what the state of a soul in such circumstances is! All that we can possibly say about it, gives but a very feeble, faint representation of it; it is inexpressible and inconceivable: For "who knows the power of God's anger?"

How dreadful is the state of those that are daily and hourly in the danger of this great wrath and infinite misery! But this is the dismal case of every soul in this congregation that has not been born again, however moral and strict, sober and religious, they may otherwise be. Oh that you would consider it, whether you be young or old! There is reason to think, that there are many in this congregation now hearing this discourse, that will actually be the subjects of this very misery to all eternity. We know not who they are, or in what seats they sit, or what thoughts they now have. It may be they are now at ease, and hear all these things without much disturbance, and are now flattering themselves that they are not the persons, promising themselves that they shall escape. If we knew that there was one person, and but one, in the whole congregation, that was to be the subject of this misery, what an awful thing would it be to think of! If we knew who it was, what an awful sight would it be to see such a person! How might all the rest of the congregation lift up a lamentable and bitter cry over him! But, alas! instead of one, how many is it likely will remember this discourse in Hell? And it would be a wonder, if some that are now present should not be in Hell in a very short time, even before this year is out. And it would be no wonder if some persons, that now sit here, in some seats of this meeting-house, in health, quiet and secure, should be there before tomorrow morning.

Those of you that finally continue in a natural condition, that shall keep out of Hell longest, will be there in a little time! Your damnation does not slumber; it will come swiftly, and, in all probability, very suddenly upon many of you. You have reason to wonder that you are not already in Hell. It is doubtless the case of some whom you have seen and known, that never deserved Hell more than you, and that heretofore appeared as likely to have been now alive as you. Their case is past all hope; they are crying in extreme misery and perfect despair; but here you are in the land of the living and in the house of God, and have an opportunity to obtain salvation. What would not those poor damned hopeless souls give for one day's opportunity such as you now enjoy!

And now you have an extraordinary opportunity, a day wherein Christ has thrown the door of mercy wide open, and stands in calling and crying with a loud voice to poor sinners; a day wherein many are flocking to him, and pressing into the kingdom of God. Many are daily coming from the east, west, north and south; many that were very lately in the same miserable condition that you are in, are now in a happy state, with their hearts filled with love to him who has loved them, and washed them from their sins in his own blood, and rejoicing in hope of the glory of God. How awful is it to be left behind at such a day! To see so many others feasting, while you are pining and perishing! To see so many rejoicing and singing for joy of heart, while you have cause to mourn for sorrow of heart, and howl for vexation of spirit! How can you rest one moment in such a condition? Are not your souls as precious as the souls of the people at Suffield, where they are flocking from day to day to Christ?

Are there not many here who have lived long in the world, and are not to this day born again? and so are aliens from the commonwealth of Israel, and have done nothing ever since they have lived, but treasure up wrath against the day of wrath? Oh, sirs, your case, in an especial manner, is extremely dangerous. Your guilt and hardness of heart is extremely great. Do you not see how generality persons of your years are passed over and left, in the present remarkable and wonderful dispensation of God's mercy? You had need to consider yourselves, and awake thoroughly out of sleep. You cannot bear the fierceness and wrath of the infinite God. And you, young men, and young women, will you neglect this precious season which you now enjoy, when so many others of your age are renouncing all youthful vanities, and flocking to Christ? You especially have now an extraordinary opportunity; but if you neglect it, it will soon be with you as with those persons who spent all the precious days of youth in sin, and are now come to such a dreadful pass in blindness and hardness. And you, children, who are unconverted, do not you know that you are going down to Hell, to bear the dreadful wrath of that God, who is now angry with you every day and every night? Will you be content to be the children of the devil, when so many other children in the land are converted, and are become the holy and happy children of the King of kings?

And let every one that is yet out of Christ, and hanging over the pit of Hell, whether they be old men and women, or middle aged, or young people, or little children, now hearken to the loud calls of God's word and providence. This acceptable year of the Lord, a day of such great favor to some, will doubtless be a day of as remarkable vengeance to others. Men's hearts harden, and their guilt increases apace at such a day as this, if they neglect their souls; and never was there so great danger of such persons being given up to hardness of heart and blindness of mind. God seems now to be hastily gathering in his elect in all parts of the land; and probably the greater part of adult persons that ever shall be saved, will be brought in now in a little time, and that it will be as it was on the great out-pouring of the Spirit upon the Jews in the apostles' days; the election will obtain, and the rest will be blinded. If this should be the case with you, you will eternally curse this day, and will curse the day that ever you were born, to see such a season of the pouring out of God's Spirit, and will wish that you had died and gone to hell before you had seen it. Now undoubtedly it is, as it was in the days of John the Baptist, the axe is in an extraordinary manner laid at the root of the trees, that every tree which brings not forth good fruit, may be hewn down and cast into the fire.

Therefore, let every one that is out of Christ, now awake and fly from the wrath to come. The wrath of Almighty God is now undoubtedly hanging over a great part of this congregation. Let every one fly out of Sodom: "Haste and escape for your lives, look not behind you, escape to the mountain, lest you be consumed."